Why Travel?

A Way of Being,
A Way of Seeing

BILL THOMPSON

"As an arts and travel writer, book review editor and author, Bill Thompson's experience and range of expertise is invaluable to me. He writes with verve, clear authority and knowledge."

– Nathalie Dupree, James Beard Award-winning author and TV host

"Travel is always something we've wanted to do more of … when the children are older, when we retire, etc. But Bill Thompson's *Why Travel?* makes me feel a sense of urgency. It's not just a want; travel is a need for adventurous, contemplative or creative spirits. Bill's photographs alone have me packing our bags."

– Nicole Seitz, author of The Cage-maker

"Bill Thompson's passion for travel and his love of good books are matched, thankfully, by his ability to express that enthusiasm in well-crafted paragraphs that bring his subjects to sparkling life. Read a book review by Thompson and try to keep away from the bookstore. Read a travel story and try to avoid a series of quick Google entries. You can't do it."

– Adam Parker, Arts & Culture editor,
Book Page Editor of The Post and Courier of Charleston

All photos by Bill Thompson

Praise for "Art and Craft: Thirty Years on the Literary Beat"

"Taken one by one, the pieces in Bill Thompson's first collection spotlight his matchless gifts: an active, fluent intelligence; a talent for listening and taking artists on their own terms; and a scope that honors both the local and far-flung. Together, they conjure up the Thompson era, a golden thirty-year span when each week brought a fresh bulletin from the cultural front."

– Catherine Holmes

"Thompson's own literary style is as smooth and inviting as that of many of the authors he has written about."

– Free Times

"Bill Thompson has for what seems forever been the Lowcountry's chronicler of books, good and bad, big and small, and this book bears testament to the great good work on behalf of the word he's been doing all these decades. This is a terrific compendium of publishing history and criticism, not to mention a joy to read!"

– Bret Lott, best-selling author of "Jewel"

"From fiction and biography to books about travel, history, crime, television, the Charleston Renaissance, the environment—his range is wide. What's more, the essays are just plain fun to read."

– Josephine Humphreys, best-selling author of "Rich in Love"

"To all my fellow sojourners, past, present, and future."

Contents

Foreword

by Ben McC. Moïse

For years I've spent hours on end sitting around my kitchen table with my friend Bill Thompson while lowering levels of bottles of fine Cabernet, marveling over stories of sojourns across the width and breadth of the planet and hearing of his plans for the next great adventure to places I had never thought of. Out of those kitchen table forays, if he divulged any great secrets which were key to having an enjoyable trip they would be, "don't be afraid and be prepared."

I was always envious, because Bill regularly launched forth on these personal voyages of discovery bringing back fascinating details of the natural and built landscape, the food and sometimes interesting stories about people he ran into along the way. He also captured evidence of his "discoveries" in wonderful illustrative photographs, which revealed the delights and sometimes travails of his peregrinations.

In years past, Bill wrote of his journeys as part of his multi-layered capacity as travel writer, book review editor and movie critic for the *Charleston Post and Courier*. Also sharing an interest in travel, I had the opportunity to visit several of the areas he wrote about and was frequently astonished at the depth of his perspectives and reliable information, which certainly gave me a more knowledgeable background and keener appreciation of the cultural and historic sites I was visiting.

In one passage Bill counsels that the more comfortable, well-beaten path maybe isn't as bad as it is made out to be — that is, "touristy" — but it is not the same experience as turning down a less traveled route and sometimes being confronted by a little serendipity. Bill did take those less traveled routes. I knew that from listening to his stories told around the kitchen table and you will too after reading of his travel adventures written on the pages of this book.

Prologue

L illian Smith, the great novelist and social critic, crystallized a philosophy of travel in a simple principle. She understood that as we venture out into the world, no journey transports us very far that does not also explore the world within. The why of travel is at least as important as the what or the where.

To that end, this is as much a why-to book as a how-to.

Why *do* we travel? Why should we? How can we make a journey more rewarding and meaningful? Let's begin with what traits constitute a born traveler, those that come closest to assuring that one's time and money are well spent and the most memorable experiences obtained. Flexibility and resilience are indispensable, as are curiosity, intelligence, an open mind, a hunger for new vistas and, in some cases, a certain toughness.

We must also have, or make, the time.

The sad fact is that with much travel, by the time one is getting a feel for the rhythm of a place, it's time to leave. This is particularly true of the average 10-day to two-week excursions cross-country or abroad. Is it better to focus your energies on one place – a great city, say – and explore it to the full, to choose one locale as the hub of a trip and venture along its spokes, or to see as many towns and nations as one can cram into a short period, having a wider (if shallower) experience? That depends on the traveler, of course. At various times, you may utilize all three strategies for a fortnight trip or longer.

It can be argued, persuasively, that slow is better than fast. But not always. You can make a good case for the reverse as well.

Do I advocate travel for its own sake? By all means. But heed the words of the great travel writer, Jan Morris, lest it feel like an obligation: "Travel, which was once either a necessity or an adventure, has become very largely a commodity, and from all sides we are persuaded into thinking that it is a social requirement, too." Discard that state of mind whenever you sense it surfacing, for the vagaries of fashion and keeping up with the Joneses are not worthy reasons to travel. A traveler's destination is not so much a place, but a new way of seeing things. Travel is not only about where you go; it's about what you bring back. Human nature being what it is, what a traveler carries back is profoundly influenced by those beliefs and values he or she carries in.

One mentality to cultivate is receptiveness. Leave preconceptions and cultural biases out of your suitcase. A true traveler does not succumb to living in a gated community of the mind, preferring contact only with those of the same economic class, tastes and political outlook, either at home or on the move. You cannot help but meet a wider, deeper cross-section of people when away from home – although one hopes you enjoy diversity of acquaintances there as well.

Getting along with people around the country or across the seas means extending to everyone that fundamental global currency: respect. Give it, get it. There is no substitute. You'll be surprised what doors it opens, what helping hands grasp yours.

The sources of information you use can be pivotal. While it is a good idea to stay abreast of the political climate, health concerns or crime in a place you plan to visit, choose up-to-date travel guides and strong magazine or newspaper reportage over what you hear on TV news, notwithstanding such occasionally excellent programs as the late Anthony Bourdain's or Rick Steves' (whose guidebooks also are among the most useful). And don't be overly swayed by U.S. State Department reports, which, though helpful, tend toward the apocalyptic. You'd be apprehensive about going to New York or New Orleans after reading one of these, much less to Bangkok, Quito or Mozambique.

You won't find an abundance of travel websites listed herein, mainly for two reasons: The sheer number of them can be daunting, and because even some of the good ones appear and disappear so quickly, with a how-to emphasis that risks being obsolete in a matter of months.

It is important to bear in mind that while not every trip is going to be sensational – snafus happen, and some experiences are simply unremarkable – even journeys that don't go as planned can be valuable, perhaps even more so. Again, the power of flexibility. Many trips that were not especially memorable at the time remain with me in interesting and useful ways.

A word on technologies

Smart phones and other such devices potentially can be lifesavers, tools for heightened efficiency, finding directions, booking reservations, or getting urgent questions answered quickly and on the fly. Overuse makes them an encumbrance, gadgets that insulate you from experience, keeping you at arm's length not only from the people around you but from the immediate stimuli of your surroundings. Employ these tools judiciously, not obsessively.

Most of us have been there, the crossroads between experiencing a travel destination through the senses and attempting to capture it in images. There's no reason that one can't augment the other, but too often travelers with a penchant for the camera wind up enjoying a place second hand.

As the late Susan Sontag wrote, to collect photos is to collect the world. Yet she also cautioned that at its most shallow and uncomprehending, travel becomes merely "a strategy for accumulating photographs."

We all want more of our journeys than that.

There's always a risk that our enthusiasm for photography can take over. When it does, we can become spectators to our own experience. I plead guilty to just such a temptation. With my love of landscape and architectural photography, both the wilderness and urban streets find me whipping out my trusty Canon at every new vista, adding a photographic notch to my belt. It is a challenge to rein myself in, absorb what I'm seeing with my own eyes and truly *inhabit the moment*.

But it's not so simple a matter as resisting the urge. Rather, it's a balancing act (or tug-of-war) between two impulses. On the one hand, as celebrated photographer Annie Leibovitz has said, there's no off switch for having and processing perceptions. "One doesn't stop seeing," she observed. "One doesn't stop *framing*. It doesn't turn off and turn on. It's on all the time."

True, though the traveler would do well to heed the advice of the great portrait photographer Yousuf Karsh: "Look and think before opening the shutter. The heart and mind are the true lens of the camera."

By all means, learn your camera's features and savor what it offers to the traveler, not least the power to arrest a fleeting moment in time and give memory the added, indelible dimension of a visual record. Months or years removed from a trip, these images can be vivid reminders of the small details.

If photography can be obsessive, the smart phone has an even greater capacity to divert. Too often I see travelers lost in their view screens, oblivious to the world around them. I recall a young woman at a café on Santorini, the Greek island blessed with some of the most glorious views in the world. As I sat there for more than an hour enjoying a carafe of wine, occasionally I'd glance her way. Her gaze never seemed to leave her smart phone. Why would someone devote considerable time and expense to come to this oasis of beauty, only to ignore the surroundings they were privileged to be in? To keep up with their e-mail? Please.

Overuse and over-reliance make technology an impediment, gadgets that serve to insulate you from experience, keeping you at arm's length not only from fellow humans but from the immediate stimuli of your surroundings — the flora and fauna and architectural/artistic wonders that are so much a part of memorable travel.

So, my advice is simple: Employ all these modern technological marvels judiciously, not obsessively. Or leave them at home. After all, travelers got along just fine without them for thousands of years. With a bit of planning and foresight, you still can.

Seasoned travelers always will benefit from advance study, networking, and planning. And those preparing to set foot on the path for the first time should embrace the excitement of the new. Recall the old adage, trite but true: A journey begins with a single step. Take it.

(**Author's note:** Each chapter's introductory essay represents new material. As all of the travel articles following the essays were previously published, some of the information regarding individual restaurants, hotels and attractions may be out of date. But one purpose of those articles was to take a "snapshot" of a place as it existed at that point in time.)

CHAPTER 1
Leaving the Cocoon

Leaving the Cocoon

"One doesn't discover new lands without consenting
to lose sight of the shore."

– Andre Gide in *Les faux-monnayeurs* (*The Counterfeiters*, 1925)

You need not be Paul Theroux, much less Marco Polo, to answer the call of travel. It's not about distances traversed or the number of places visited, though these can be touchstones of a sort. Rather, it's about how much you are willing to shed the comforting cocoon of normalcy and the familiar to immerse yourself in new experience, leaving your psychological and prejudicial baggage behind.

Expect difference. Embrace it.

Setting out in this way can be a great source of energy as well as resilience, a gateway not only to discovery, but to re-discovery, as in one's innocence (abroad or otherwise). Change is inevitable in the process of travel. Much of the time, you don't even have to work at it. It's a kind of osmosis.

If you are inexperienced, take it in small steps, gradually expanding your horizons and gaining confidence in your ability to adapt, to apprehend, to try on new ideas and see how they fit. Be bold. Don't confuse caution with timidity. Yes, things can be confusing, even daunting at times, but if a callow college kid can backpack all over the map, seeing the world on a shoestring, you can manage a portion of the unknown.

There's something to be said for exploring your own region to start. But as your reach expands, so will your ambitions. One of your first major surprises may greet you not in transit, but upon your return. Home is never quite the same place you left. It can't be, because travel activates a shift, from slight or profound, in how you perceive those you've met, by the influences of other travelers, by witnessing how challenges in your country have been resolved elsewhere.

Though our planet is immense, the power of travel in the modern age shrinks its vastness even as it offers inexhaustible opportunities. Travel also enables us to integrate our consciousness with a larger one: The joy of finding one's self as a citizen of the world.

Explore that sense of citizenship by trying new things, not least new foods and new activities.

From a practical standpoint, there are a number of fundamental steps to take before you go anywhere, particularly if it's abroad. Don't forget to ask your physician or public health department what immunizations and medical records are required or recommended for your destination. Do your research! Get a working grasp of local customs. This applies as much to Texas or Maine as it does to foreign lands. Master a few key phrases of the language.

When you arrive, adopt a cheerful and well-mannered tone. Be friendly. Be patient. Be able to laugh at yourself when you screw up. A sense of humor can carry you a long way. And you do everyone a favor by leaving a good impression.

Establish a budget. Know what you want to see and do at your destination(s) but keep your itinerary flexible enough to let serendipity take a hand. However tempting it may be, don't try to do too much in too short a time. Purchase travel insurance (you never know) from a reputable company.

Make sure your passport is up to date. Make a copy of it and keep it in a separate place. Ditto for copies of your itinerary and other travel documents, one of which you should leave with a family member or friend. Take an adapter so you can recharge your phone overseas. A good camera is indispensable. If you don't already know how to employ the manual settings on your camera, learn before you depart, or carry a small cheat sheet on a piece of paper.

Pack as light as possible. Above all, have a good pair of walking shoes for city strolls and/or hiking boots for the great outdoors. Include a change of clothes in your carry-on luggage, just in case checked luggage flies elsewhere.

Go with your gut as well as your head. Be aware of your immediate surroundings. If something doesn't feel right, examine the situation. If it still doesn't feel right, don't do it. Wear a security purse or wallet out of sight and consider carrying a "dummy" billfold to foil potential thieves in pickpocket-prone places. You're not being paranoid. You're just being sensible.

They can be frustrating, but don't let minor missteps or delays get under your skin. They go with the territory.

Travel is a privilege. It is good to remember that today's average traveler, armed with only a modest income and varied degrees of acumen, has the ability to do what only princes and potentates could do in earlier eras. Quite something, that.

Don't make a fetish of it, but try to make the most of every minute. *Inhabit the moment.* You may never come this way again.

Travel Stories
Miami Rhapsody (2003)

Miami Beach, Fla. — They sit there, languorously, sleek as seals. Latin music throbs in the background. The woman is lovely, elegant, the man darkly handsome, smoldering. But does he look appraisingly into her eyes? No. Does she gaze provocatively at him through discreetly lowered lashes? No.

They are on separate cell phones, talking to anyone but each other.

Of course, it's only 2 a.m. The night is young. They haven't even dined.

Nightspots closing? They've barely opened. The streets are a study in gridlock, choked with cars, the sidewalks so clogged with people seeing and being seen it would take you 20 minutes to walk a block. The queues outside the clubs and cafés grow longer by the minute.

There will be no letup till sunrise. Morning people need not apply.

Welcome to South Beach, summer, where searing days give way to sultry nights. Endless nights. An art deco playground where neon comes to flare and die, it is a vibrant, absurd, fascinating, self-consciously sophisticated promenade of some of the most attractive human beings on Earth, a montage of the buff and beautiful that is hip, stylish and engagingly vulgar.

While no longer an especially chic destination, for those who assay such things, it is still "trendy," and might be the finest place for people watching on the East Coast. When the sun falls into the pocket of night, South Beach's reputation as an intersection of the Americas — Central, North and South — becomes a palpable reality. It is a multicultural collision of youth and skimpy fashions, haute cuisine and hollow attitude, *joie de vivre* and social Darwinism, big money, Eurotrash and gawking tourists.

From Ocean Drive to *Española Way* to Lincoln Road, and all points between, it's a round-the-clock frolic and a testament to the modern preoccupation with body shape. You could label it Camp Augmentation, given the eye-popping array of enhanced bodies on display. For guys, there's a ceaseless catwalk of heart-stoppingly gorgeous women. For the ladies, so many sun-bronzed Adonises flex their wares that it makes Ocean Drive seem like Muscle Beach East. For gays, same thing.

The mode of dressing is provocative, to put it mildly. Beefcake and cheesecake. Nothing is worn; it is displayed. Poured on, sprayed on, barely on, little is left to the imagination. And one way of the other, it is presumed you will have a tan, natural or acquired. The melanin impoverished stick out like banana popsicles in a forest of fudge bars.

But the singular signpost of SoBe style is the cellphone, the new century's principal affectation, universally affixed to the lobes like a burbling techno-earring.

Who exactly are they talking to at 4 a.m., a friend in a different bar on another street?

Pastel Palette

The one-square-mile Art Deco District, its buildings dating from the 1920s to the 1950s, was long a scene of abandonment or dreary disrepair. Happily, this architectural treasure was saved and revitalized in the 1980s, thanks to some visionary transplants and locals (many of them restaurateurs).

Infused with new energy, today the area owns the distinction of being the nation's first 20th-century district to be listed on the National Register of Historic Places, numbering some 800 buildings on its rolls.

A great introductory walk along the district, which stretches from 1st to 23rd streets, centers on the 10-block segment from 5th to 15th streets, much of it bordered by palm-fringed Lummus Park, gateway to the surf.

Start on the south end of the park, savoring the deco stalwarts running chockablock along Ocean Drive. The aesthetics swing from splendidly tacky to understated classic, riotously colored to sedate. The Cardozo, the Leslie, and the Clevelander Hotels are particular standouts. And look for Casa Casuarina (Ocean Drive at 11th), the ornate three-story palazzo once owned by the late Gianni Versace.

A favored locale for lunch on Ocean Drive is the News Café, a well-placed nook to catch your breath and check out the passing panorama.

Each of the three principal arteries running parallel to the beach — Washington Avenue, Collins Avenue and Ocean Drive — is decorated with deco restorations or recreations. Cafés line each, though Ocean Drive is billed as the city's heartbeat. But its soul, locals say, is romantic, lushly planted Lincoln Road, a nine-block-long malled area with 300 boutiques, galleries, cafés and clubs flanking its palm- and fountain-festooned length. The road trends a bit older, more urbane, comfortable in its casual glamour, with less bustle and posturing (though not by much) than Ocean Drive.

People spill into and out of the street at all hours, the mood convivial. Among the prime watering holes are Locando Sibilla (also a fine restaurant), the Van

Dyke Café (the chief live jazz venue in South Florida resides upstairs) and the racy, risqué Touch.

Throughout Miami Beach, restaurants cover all bases, from high-end Italian and Caribbean/Nouvelle fusion to Cuban and various permutations of South American and Asian, their alluring young hawkers beckoning you in. While not inexpensive, by any measure, they are more or less fairly priced because of ferocious competition.

Those inclined toward tradition, and visiting between October and May, should make a pilgrimage up the beach to fabled Joe's Stone Crab, where Ian Fleming's persnickety alter ego, James Bond, had the greatest meal of his life.

People in the streets are grouped in couples or in pods of various sizes, which makes it devilishly hard to meet someone if you are unattached, or get a seat at a café, outside of the bar. Singles, in the sense of individuals alone, are as rare as Swedes. If not frowned upon, they are not exactly courted either. Getting that appealing table at a restaurant or sidewalk café is a tall order when you're going solo. But it can be done.

Med Flavor

Española Way is the coziest street around, a gas-lamped Alhambra whose Mediterranean Revival charm is expressed in galleries, shops, eateries and weekend bazaars, all anchored by the old, atmospheric Clay Hotel and International Youth Hostel, which once housed a casino owned by Al Capone. No longer notorious, perhaps, but the street retains a flavor of the clandestine. While there, slip into a chaise and sip a Mojito classico, that bracing concoction of rum, lime and spearmint, with a spike of sugarcane for elan.

Across the way, on Washington Avenue, the late, late crowd will be kickin' at the Cameo, a one-time deco theater that's now a dance club. It starts smoking a little later than most.

Whatever your taste, there's a place.

We also hear that there's a beach. You know, sand, sun, turquoise water, cabanas, bikinis (topless and otherwise) — that sort of thing.

When you take a break from the waves, feed the mind at the Bass Museum of Art, which offers a refreshing (and edifying) diversion on a blistering day. As does the Jewish Museum of Florida and the Wolfsonian Foundation archive. A more sobering stop is the Holocaust Memorial.

Getting around

One can drive, here in the world's capital of Mercedes convertibles. But most choose to amble, bike or slalom about atop in-line skates. Apart from cabs and the not-always-timely Metrobus, South Beach sports the aptly named Electrowave, an electric shuttle conveyance whose "cars" stop every eight minutes, coursing through the Art Deco District's circulatory system.

The water taxis connecting Miami Beach to the mainland are gone, alas. No more picturesque cruises up the Miami River to Big Fish or Bijan. But four causeways remain. Take your car or take a bus. Just keep an eye peeled crossing Biscayne Bay. You'll spot a phalanx of private islands studded with gaudy mansions that are monuments to success, or excess (take your pick). It's "Miami Vice" all over again.

Once in metro Miami, there's the MetroMover, a free 4.4-mile elevated monorail system affording a panoramic view of the downtown. The Mover has many a desirable stop, such as lively, family oriented Bayfront Park and saucy Little Havana with its Calle Ocho district. More expensive is the Metrorail, a 21-mile elevated rapid transit system.

Room with a view

As a rule, accommodations in South Beach are pricey, especially during the winter high season, but there are secret enclaves. You can stay at The Tides, an opulent hotel on Ocean Drive, for up to $3,000 a night, or for a good bit less at the tastefully modern Hotel Astor, whose bar and grill is a showpiece. On the other hand, a deluxe hotel room at the aforementioned Clay can be had for as little as $84 a night (2016 rates), with most of the expected amenities.

Those opting for a dorm-style hostel can manage for as little as $25 a night. Seriously, how much time do you plan to spend in your room, anyway?

Of course, there's another Miami Beach, the one populated by residents. Take the time to taste it. Flamingo Park is one nexus, around which are tucked tree-shaded neighborhoods of delightful homes and apartment buildings, many in the deco style.

The Miami area is many things (What must it have been like to have grown up here rather than in, say, Kansas?). And there are aspects of it that may offend. Drug culture is alive and thriving. Like all cities and tourist destinations, there is the unsavory and the objectionable. During the summer swelter, the wastage of energy beggars the imagination. It's commonplace for shops to fling wide their doors throughout operating hours, cold conditioned air wafting from the storefront into the street and enticing heat-bedraggled folk into their confines — a questionable marketing ploy, considering that everyone's doing it.

Be prepared. The heat will hammer you. Take Miamians' advice: Sweat, don't fret. And you might try wearing that Cuban standby, the guayabera, an airy shirt made of linen or cotton. Leave the top few buttons unfastened. Adopt the air of a seasoned boulevardier.

Even if you're not 23, rich and ready for action, you may never want to leave.

Scenic splendor: West Virginia (2009)

LEWISBURG, W.Va. — Talk about a split personality.

West Virginia, like Kentucky, always has been betwixt and between geographically. And perhaps psychologically. Is it Southern? Northern? Midwestern? Yes, in varying degrees, and depending on what sector of the state one calls home.

"Here's to West Virginia!" a traditional toast exults. "The most Northern of the Southern states, the most Southern of the Northern states, the most Western of the Eastern states."

In what quickly became a musical cliché, John Denver called it "almost heaven," rivaling the "Rocky Mountain high" of his first love, Colorado. Those partial to mountain terrain and grand vistas would agree, notwithstanding the hair-raising switchbacks of the Potomac Highlands, named for the river whose headwaters rise here.

West Virginia long ago was dubbed the Mountain State, and in easternmost Monongahela National Forest alone, there are 100 peaks that ascend to 4,000 feet – the Allegheny Front of the Appalachians.

Much may be said in admiration of the New River Gorge just west of Lansing, with its sheer, thousand-foot cliffs, and of such evocative state parks as Pipestem Resort, Hawk's Nest and Babcock in the southern region. But the purest expression of West Virginia's appeal may be along the verdant, 200-mile length of Route 219, winding north from the historic town of Lewisburg to Elkins. A skier's nirvana in winter, it is tailor-made for motorists, hikers and cyclists the rest of the year.

On high

With few exceptions, this drive stays within the vastness of Monongahela, which embraces 900,000 acres of woodlands and meadows, 19 campgrounds, 700 miles of hiking trails (from easy to moderate to "say your prayers") and more than 600 miles of cold-water streams sending their siren song to anglers. Of particular note is an optional 43-mile side trip through the national forest along routes 150 and 55 West to Richwood, accessed almost halfway up Route 219 near Marlinton.

Also known as the Highland Scenic Highway, this low-traffic road owns dramatic views of the Alleghenies (elevations range from 2,400 to 4,600 feet) and passes the bucolic Falls of Hills Creek while navigating the 36,000-acre Cranberry Wilderness Area. Wildlife in evidence include black bear, mink, bobcat, white-tailed deer, Eastern cottontail and wild turkey.

Lewisburg is an optimal starting point for several reasons. First, it is eight miles west of White Sulfur Springs, home to the famed Greenbrier Resort, looking very like a cross between the White House and an antebellum Southern mansion. Lewisburg itself has undeniable charm, however keyed it may be to well-heeled patrons from the Greenbrier. With a 236-acre National Historic District, the town boasts handsome homes and churches (one erected in 1796), boutiques, cafés, coffee houses and the venerable General Lewis Inn and Restaurant.

Once an outpost of the Confederacy, Lewisburg still bears the scars of war on some of its buildings. Nearby Big Sewell Mountain was occupied by Gen. Robert E. Lee and his troops during a campaign in 1861. Just north of Lewisburg lies a nexus of three state parks: Beartown, Watoga (the state's largest) and Droop Mountain Battlefield, the last reflecting just how deeply divided West Virginia was by the conflict. Some 30,000 men shouldered arms for the Union, 7,500 for the South. The defining and final battle in West Virginia occurred Nov. 6, 1863, with federal forces outflanking the Confederates on the peak and driving them home.

Watoga's Arrowhead Trail is an admirable introduction to that park's jumble of ridges, hollows and second-growth forest, and the nearby town of Hillsboro is notable as the birthplace of novelist Pearl S. Buck ("The Good Earth"), the first American woman to be awarded the Nobel Prize in Literature.

Crown jewels

Continue on 219 North to the outskirts of Marlinton, where ambitious hikers can tackle the 75-mile Greenbrier River Trail, which traces an old rail bed of the Chesapeake and Ohio Railway through picturesque countryside. Others will want to continue on to the Highland Scenic Highway turnoff and the all-season resort at Snowshoe Mountain. Thereafter, the drive meanders past the Gaudineer Scenic Area en route to Elkins.

At Elkins, leave 219 and pick up Route 33 East toward the Stuart Recreation Area and Bickle Knob, both of which are worth a morning's or afternoon's jaunt. From there, stay on 33 southwest to the Spruce Knob-Seneca Rocks National Recreation Area. Here, the craggy, 425-million-year-old Rocks — "like like the backbone of a gigantic prehistoric dinosaur," in the words of naturalist Norma Jean Venable — tower 960 feet above North Fork Valley, and lofty, 4,861-foot Spruce Knob stakes its claim as West Virginia's highest peak.

The U.S. Forest Service also maintains the 25-mile North Fork Mountain Trail, a prime spot for spying raptors riding the thermal updrafts. Some say these birds of prey harbor the spirits of Seneca braves who, wooing the Native American princess Snowbird, were challenged by her to climb to the top to prove themselves worthy.

Next, retrace your steps along Route 33 and take Route 32 North. Just a few miles away are, arguably, the crown jewels of the Potomac Highlands: Canaan Valley State Park, Blackwater Falls State Park and Dolly Sods Wilderness and Scenic Area.

Cradled by the Alleghenies, Canaan Valley reminded 18th-century fur traders of the biblical Canaan, a land of milk and honey. Wary hunters had a differing opinion, thanks to the threat of bears, pumas, tangled growth and dangerous cliffs. The valley inhabits the largest and highest (3,200 feet) plateau east of the Rockies, and is one of the most popular ski resorts in the state. But there are ample opportunities for hiking, mountain biking and canoeing.

Overlook the throngs of tourists and you can savor the sight of majestic Blackwater Falls. The distinctive red-brown torrent is stained by leaching from upcountry hemlocks and spruce, while blooming rhododendron limns the canyon edges in season. Evade the crowds by getting on Canaan Loop Road at the visitor center and following it to the terminus. There, a short trail festooned with mountain laurel leads to one of the most splendid panoramas of the East: Lindy Point Overlook.

Campers, hikers and mountain bikers will find much to appreciate in the area.

A sweeping grass bald (treeless area) on the edge of the Allegheny Plateau, Dolly Sods casts an eerie, otherworldly spell. Once used as grazing lands, the 2,400-acre scenic area is approached via routes 24 and 11 southeast of Red Creek. A walk here feels like an amble way out West.

One of the advantages of West Virginia hiking is how exceptionally well marked the trailheads are, not to mention how well the trails themselves are maintained. This sort of conscientiousness seems to typify the state as a whole, which owns a pride and a friendliness that's hard to miss.

CHAPTER 2

Seeing (North)
America first

Seeing (North) America first

*"Travel does what good novelists also do to the life of everyday,
placing it like a picture in a frame or a gem in its setting, so that
the intrinsic qualities are made more clear."*
– Freya Stark

Why, when so many exotic destinations beckon in an expansive age of travel, would North Americans be counseled to experience their own continent first? Because it is huge, it is diverse, it is extraordinarily interesting. Because it has many cultures, many landscapes in one, relatively close at hand.

Many who style themselves globetrotters have flung themselves far across the seas, yet seldom have strayed from their region of the U.S. to explore others. A shame. When you see North America for reasons of geophysical and cultural "patriotism," as opposed to the chauvinistic kind, it can be immensely rewarding. The great cities alone bear such distinct and wide-ranging cultural differences that they harbor inexhaustible features of interest. The landscapes? Wilderness areas? As glorious as any on Planet Earth.

As the great artist Thomas Cole (1801-1848) wrote, "(American scenery) is a subject that to every American ought to be of surpassing interest; for, whether he beholds the Hudson mingling waters with the Atlantic, explores the central wilds of this vast continent, or stands on the margin of the distant Oregon, he is still in the midst of American scenery — it is his own land; its beauty, its magnificence, its sublimity — are all his; and how undeserving of such a birthright, if he can turn towards it an unobserving eye, an unaffected heart?"

Some have struck out with little more than a backpack and a case of optimism, thumbing their way cross country in a pivotal rite of passage. Others set out in an RV with all the conveniences, or flit around by airplane, train and rental car. Others go by bike, sometimes making multiple crossings in their lifetimes, a feat Bruce Weber chronicled so vividly in his recent memoir, *Life is a Wheel*.

The conveyance doesn't matter, though the route often does. It's all there for us: cityscapes and small towns, deserts and rain forests, grasslands and alpine meadows, majestic mountain ranges and rocky islands, coastlines graceful and rugged, geysers and volcanoes. From Manhattan to Malibu, the Adirondacks to the Everglades, Lake Superior to the Grand Canyon, Vancouver Island to Nova Scotia, the Oregon coast to the Louisiana Bayous, the Badlands to the Colorado Rockies, the Mississippi to the Rio Grande, Copper Canyon to Baja and the Sea of Cortez, a world awaits.

Yes, we include Mexico. And why not? In the strict sense, Mexico is no less North American, physically, than the U.S. or Canada, though it is seldom viewed this way. Those who have ventured there know that it is every bit as varied in region, terrain, climate and cultures, filled with ancient mysteries, as its neighbors to the north, and well worth exploring.

There is no better way of savoring these wonders than on foot – the oldest and perhaps best form of travel. This is how one really sees a city, simply wandering. It is also how you immerse yourself in nature. As with mountain climbing, moderate to strenuous hiking not only is a way of taking the measure of your physical limitations, but of getting out of yourself and then, with fatigue and heightened clarity, back in. But there are hikes for every taste and fitness level. Be it a day hike (with a comfy lodge or campsite at the end of the day), or backpacking over long distances, little rivals the satisfaction being self-propelled, to pause at whim, to enjoy the symphony of nature's sounds or the stillnesses that let you *absorb* your surroundings. We are, after all, part of nature too.

Walking is a meditative act, the pilgrim's mode, and the preferred transport of many of history's most revered travelers.

If you think you're too old, have to be as vigorous as an Olympian, or must buy a bunch of expensive gear to hit the trail, know that I'm in my early 70s and in pretty decent shape, yet often have been passed by many an advanced septuagenarian and young mother with a papoose on her back, sometimes in flip-flops.

Our splendid network of national parks, reserves and wildlife refuges offers a gateway to witnessing the wild and feeding the spirit, provided that — apart from the great scenic drives — you get out of the car and onto your feet.

While deep excursions into wild country can be arduous, even perilous for the unprepared (or unlucky), even short trips to the edge of the wilderness offer limitless opportunities for observation. The still-wild places are part of our heritage. Discovering the details of a place acts to make it a part of us.

There are also no end of curiosities in North America's natural realm, such as Manitoulin Island, a Canadian isle in Lake Huron that happens to be the largest freshwater lake island in the world. But its claim to fame goes beyond that. Manitoulin Island contains 108 lakes of its own, the largest being Lake Manitou, Lake Kagawong and Lake Mindemoya, each of which have islands within them. The largest of these is Lake Mindemoya's 82-acre Treasure Island, which makes it "the largest island in a lake on an island in a lake in the world." How's that for a distinction?

Perhaps you are fortunate enough to have the wild (or a reasonable approximation) at your doorstep. Those that do have the opportunity to explore a place deeply. To know intimately one mountain, one meadow, one lake, one stretch of coastline can be a life's experience.

Travel Stories
Teton grandeur (2011)

JACKSON, Wyo. – They are young and impertinent, only 10 million years old, and given to all the grandstanding of youth.

Jutting skyward from the sage-covered valley of Jackson Hole and topped by the 13,770-foot Grand Teton, the craggy, snow-capped Teton range represents a fledgling family of mountains – America's most callow – though some contain the gneiss and schist of vastly older rocks.

There are no intervening foothills. Taller than they are broad, the Grand, Middle and South Tetons seem to erupt from the flats. They form the heart of the range, rising through steep coniferous forest into alpine meadows strewn with wildflowers. But their most prominent neighbors – mounts Owen, Teewinot and Moran – are equally impressive.

Thanks to a fault-line displacement that continues to this day, the Tetons and their high desert valley have separated by some 30,000 vertical feet.

The centerpiece of the Teton wilderness is 485-square-mile Grand Teton National Park, where majestic ramparts combine with the famed wildlife viewing of the Greater Yellowstone Ecosystem to draw many of the world's top alpine adventurers – peak huggers, big-wall climbers, backcountry and free skiers – as well as such garden-variety enthusiasts as backpackers, mountain hikers and motorists.

In all the Rockies, there is no grander view. And it is fortified on all sides by a phalanx of other natural areas: the Bridger-Teton and Targhee National Forests and the 25,000-acre National Elk Refuge.

Hike it, bike it, ski it, drive it or raft down the Snake River, gazing west at the Tetons' 12 remaining glaciers. Within the park roam bison, moose, pronghorn, mule deer and elk, while black and grizzly bears, coyotes and wolves top the food chain.

A crush of powder

Early visitors this summer met with the unexpected impediment of lingering ice and snow. Even at lower elevations, some areas were still saddled with residues of one of the most prodigious winters in memory — some 700 inches of snow, or 235 percent above normal, fell on the Tetons — and avalanches remained a danger as late as mid-June. Many high-elevation hiking trails were shut down, but that left no shortage of excellent lake and canyon trails.

July and August are the most frequented and crowded months, but for many, fall is the golden time, literally and figuratively, with pleasant days, brisk nights and fewer people with whom to share the colors of autumn.

Established in 1929 and expanded by presidential decree in 1943, the compromise that resulted in the park one sees today did not emerge until 1950, after a long, acrimonious battle between the federal government and irate Wyoming politicians and landowners, a story dramatized in Ken Burns' documentary, "The National Parks."

On the road

From the moment you depart the town of Jackson heading north, the Tetons emerge, as if from an Ansel Adams image, towering above the valley (what 19th-century trappers called a "hole"). This is your corridor to Grand Teton National Park.

Two principal scenic drives embrace the park's sites and form a loop: the combined U.S. 26/191/89 and Teton Park Road, the park's "inner" route beginning at Moose Junction. Side trips intersecting with Teton Park Road include Signal Mountain Summit Road, whose two pullouts (the lower particularly) reveal the park's single most dazzling view of the entire Teton Range, Jackson Lake, the broad sweep of Jackson Hole and distant Yellowstone.

Then there is the Jenny Lake Scenic Drive, among whose delights are the jaw-dropping Cathedral Group Turnout, offering the most unobstructed panorama of the three main peaks, and a dazzling lake view turnout just south of Jenny

Lake Lodge that opens to Cascade Canyon.

Teton Park Road also provides the main access to most park trailheads and, with its wide shoulders, is tailor-made for cyclists.

Apart from the Gros Ventre Loop side trip close to Jackson, offering access to the remarkable Gros Ventre Slide, the outer route also sports two stunning overlooks facing west: Teton Point Turnout and the Snake River Overlook (a spot favored by Adams and countless other photographers). Small herds of bison, elk and pronghorn graze the flats. The river, having begun its journey in Yellowstone National Park, winds its swift, serpentine way to Idaho, passing groves of cottonwoods, aspens, willows and lodgepole pines – a roost for ospreys and bald eagles. Farther up the road at Oxbow Bend Turnout, moose and mule deer pad the thickets, while beavers, otters and muskrats go industriously about their business.

The Moose Junction (south), Jenny Lake (central) and Colter Bay (north) visitor centers harbor the customary maps and brochures, plus exhibits and up-to-date information on trail conditions. You also will obtain variations on the story of how French-Canadian beaver trappers gave the geologic sculpture of the Tetons their name, likening *les trois tetons* to a woman's bosom. Too long (and too lonely) in the wilderness, one gathers.

On foot

Trekking trails course through 200 miles of the park, along with backcountry ski routes and challenges sufficient for the most ambitious mountaineer and rock-climber.

Long, arduous hiking trails abound, with backcountry routes climbing high into the mountains and behind them. But you can just as easily get a feel for the land with a batch of worthy day hikes, most of them through rich conifer forest, such as the moderate yet spectacular Phelps Lake, Taggart Lake/Bradley Lake and Hidden Falls trails.

Want to stretch your limits a bit? Try the Surprise and Amphitheater Lakes loop, recently named the No. 1 day hike in the Rockies by the hikers' Internet oracle www.gorp.com. All offer remarkable views and plenty of wildlife. But learn to be bear aware, and keep your distance from even the least threatening creature.

For a bracing ride to a perch atop the range, and access to the Teton Crest Trail, climb aboard the Jackson Hole Aerial Tram, which glides from the valley's 6,000-foot elevation to the summit of 10,450-foot Rendezvous Peak.

The array of private adventure jaunts and guided tours are too numerous to mention, as are lodging possibilities, but they can be accessed via www.grand. teton.national-park.com and www.gorp.com.

In town ... giddyup

Being the gateway to fashionable ski resorts in winter and a madhouse of park-goers in July and August – the warmest, driest months – the town of Jackson (pop. 8,500-plus, minus the visitors) is a tourist town of wall-to-wall galleries (some quite impressive), souvenir shops, purveyors of Western garb, outdoor outfitters, tour companies and often pricey restaurants.

If you decide against the park's more bucolic lodgings, Jackson is a fine base camp for venturing out. It's a lively little town, and much of its history can be traced in photographs that adorn the lobby of the venerable Wort Hotel.

On the outskirts of Jackson, facing the immense National Elk Refuge, winter feeding ground for the largest migratory elk herd (7,000-10,000) in North America, is the exemplary National Museum of Wildlife Art (2820 Rungius Rd., 307-733-5771).

Howdy, neighbor

It is almost impossible to regard Grand Teton and Yellowstone national parks as separate entities, though they are, joined by the John D. Rockefeller Jr. Memorial Parkway (89/191).

If the former is more "compact," with loftier, more magnificent mountains, the latter owns an even greater concentration of (visible) wildlife to go with its geothermal wonders. The landscapes are no less picturesque, at least on the greener east side of Yellowstone's Grand Loop Road.

Yet being among the throngs visiting the two parks in early summer, it's hard to escape the feeling of being part of a growing problem. The national parks always have served a dual design: to sustain the land and its wildlife, but also to preserve these natural spaces as something akin to outdoor museum exhibits for human appreciation.

Human pressure here can be daunting. Even these vastnesses are damaged and fragile pockets of the wild, with many endangered animal populations, among them the once ubiquitous grizzlies. Leaving the smallest possible footprint is the least one can do.

Getting a French Fix (2013)

QUEBEC CITY, Quebec — It is doubtful that even Samuel de Champlain, revered "Father of New France," ever savored such a feast.

Certainly no mere trapper or voyageur ever sat down to boar and wild caribou rillette with cranberry chutney, warm goat cheese salad with maple vinaigrette, and a Lac St-Jean pie filled with wild meats accompanied by a pheasant and bison casserole.

Yet these are traditional Quebecois dishes: hearty, muscular fare that insulates against long, bitter winters and compels the diner to pat his stomach with profound satisfaction.

Wherever one lives in Canada, it is to the province of Quebec one comes to enjoy such old-fashioned dishes, not least the ubiquitous, somewhat daunting poutine, a concoction beloved of the locals that consists of a mound of homemade french fries topped by cheese curd and a blanket of thick brown gravy.

"Quebec," or "Kebec" in the original Algonquin, means "where the river narrows," referring to the mighty St. Lawrence, a waterway almost 60 miles across at its widest point. A steady diet of old Quebecois food, alas, could mean "where the arteries narrow."

Which is why a visit to, say, Aux Anciens Canadiens, a mecca of traditional cuisine tucked into the historic district's oldest (1676) house at the corner of Rue Saint-Louis and Rue de Jardins, generally is reserved for a special occasion.

European flavor

It is a cliché to call Quebec City "Europe at our doorstep," but the sobriquet is not wrong.

From its cobblestone streets to its graceful architecture, the city's Old Town (Vieux-Quebec) harbors not only an evocative Old World appearance but a palpable European feel, albeit infused with North American sensibilities.

The province of Quebec was founded on July 3, 1608, by Champlain, the great navigator, cartographer, explorer, geographer and diplomat. And it is from the site of an abandoned Iroquoian settlement called Stadacona that "Canada" derives its name.

Quebec City itself is among the most venerable European settlements in the Western Hemisphere, with Vieux-Quebec owning the distinction of being the only fortified city north of Mexico whose walls still stand (guarded by many a ceremonial cannon).

Preceding Champlain, French explorer Jacques Cartier erected a fort at the site in 1535. Quebec City served as the staging area for raids against New England during the French and Indian War. After several decisive battles, New France, and the city of Quebec, were ceded to Great Britain in 1763.

American attempts to "liberate" Quebec City during the Revolutionary War came to nought. Yankee designs on annexing Canadian lands in 1812 also failed. Wary of another U.S. incursion, however, the Quebecois began construction of the Citadelle of Quebec in 1820. Still used by the military, it remains a prime tourist attraction.

Charm to burn

Today, Quebec City is home to 516,622 citizens, with a metro population of 765,706, the province's second largest city after Montreal. Its most impressive physical feature is its promontory, Cap-Diamant (Cape Diamond).

With Levis, a town on the opposite (south) bank, it defines the river's narrows. The Laurentian Mountains, among the oldest on the planet, pass by to the north of the city.

Vieux-Quebec is divided between Upper Town atop Cap-Diamant, with its high stone ramparts; Lower Town at shore level beneath the promontory; and the gently undulating Plains of Abraham, at whose terminus is the impressive Musee National des Beaux-Arts (National Museum of Fine Arts of Quebec).

Joining Upper and Lower Towns is the Escalier, otherwise known as the "neck-breaking steps," or for those averse, the $2-a-ride Funicular, or cliff railway.

The broad Terrasse Dufferin (Dufferin Terrace), a walkway along the edge of the cliff, offers beautiful views of the St. Lawrence River. But the most memorable sight may be directly behind it, Château Frontenac, the skyline-dominating grand hotel (designed by American architect Bruce Price), that is the city's signature image.

Top or bottom, the old city exerts its seductive charms. And the best way to discover it is on foot. Strolling is a delightful experience, but those unaccustomed to climbing stairs and hills should invest in a good pair of walking shoes.

With little industry to speak of, aside from the export of electricity, Quebec City relies on its tourism. And it features a remarkable array of restaurants, from such Upper Town temples of haute cuisine as Panache, Initiale and Le

Cremaillere to dark, sumptuous bistros like Voo Doo Grill and Cafe Sirocco that dot the youth-favored avenue Grande Allee. Of the many convivial pubs, D'Orsay and Saint-Alexandre stand out.

A thriving farmers market on the marina also offers fresh, locally grown produce.

Aside from its famous Petit Champlain district, which begins at the base of the Funicular, Lower Town also is the setting for Place Royale, a showcase of preserved 17th- and 18th-century buildings.

Quebec City's highest concentration of art galleries and boutiques are in Lower Town, as well as the Notre-Dame-des-Victoires church (oldest in the city) and the much-admired Musee de la Civilisation (Museum of Civilization).

Porte St-Louis and Porte St-Jean are the main gates through the walls leading to and from the modern section of downtown.

Where to stay

One may lodge at the imposing Château Frontenac, or, for considerably less money, at any of a number of small but well-appointed inns that reside in its shadow.

Nearby are such attractions as Parc Aquarium du Quebec; Montmorency Falls Park near Beauport, whose majestic 270-foot falls marks the confluence of the Montmorency and St. Lawrence rivers; the Basilica Sainte-Anne de-Beaupré in the town of Sainte-Anne; and the Mont-Sainte-Anne ski resort.

But if you are thinking to escape the heat with a summer jaunt to Quebec, think again. Summers are quite warm and occasionally hot, often humid until the end of August, while spring and fall are more clement.

Fall foliage generally peaks the last week of September or the first week in October. Winter is best left to locals, skiers and devotees of the city's spectacular Winter Carnival celebration.

Don't speak French? Fret not. The simple gesture or saying "Bonjour" or "Bonsoir" is usually sufficient to win a local's favor, and they will instantly segue to English.

While you, brave soul, sample the poutine.

CHAPTER 3

On and Off the Beaten Path

On and Off the Beaten Path

"We travel not to escape life, but for life not to escape us."
– Anonymous

For the longest time, I styled myself a traveler, not a tourist, who I regarded as someone enthralled by the conventional package tour, inescapably encased in his/her own culture and more or less blind to the real world spread out before us. Benumbed. I liked to think I embodied, at least much of the time, that better half of the remark, "A traveler doesn't know where he's going; a tourist doesn't know where he's been."

To some, not least my best friend, this stance had the whiff of pretension and snobbery. I claimed otherwise, insisting it was all about being discerning, preferring the serendipitous and unexpected – real experience – over the predictable, manufactured and cushy. The backdoor rather than the front, so to speak.

But over time I began to see the preoccupation with tourist-avoidance and off-the-beaten-path travel, however seductive or advantageous, as unnecessarily limiting. (And, to be honest, discomforts and unpleasant surprises are less and less on my agenda as I grow older).

Consider: The "beaten path" becomes that for a reason, and to dismiss that route as too touristy or tacky or superficial is misguided if applied too strenuously. You can deny yourself many arresting moments by rejecting the tried and true, especially in the great cities of the world, which, among other things, tend to present many free options.

One of our more perceptive travel writers, Doug Mack, has called the beaten path "the crossroads of the world," and I agree, noting that the stereotype of the clueless American tourist singularly lacking in taste or manners or genuine curiosity is just that, a stereotype. You're liable to meet folks on the "tourist track" that are intelligent, sophisticated, amiable and as interested in plumbing the local culture as you are. And there's no reason you cannot dig beneath the surface even where the track is worn. There is something to be said for rubbing shoulders with fellow travelers, as well as with the locals.

Frankly, unless you're spending the summer in a rented Italian villa where you shop and dine in the neighboring village each day, the reality is that you are not very likely to forge a relationship with members of the indigenous population overnight. They are too busy going about their own business. Just think of how it would feel if a visitor from a foreign land was eager to establish a connection with you in the middle of your workday. Flattering, yes, but also disruptive. You may not meet as many "colorful" characters as you might in the hinterlands, but you will enjoy the company and observations of those you do meet, many of whom will be visitors from countries other than your own.

This is not to say that a person should not be selective — some tourists are obnoxious, living down to the cliché — but one can tolerate the most claustrophobic crush of people and enjoy even the most prefabricated Disney-esque sights with a sense of humor, a taste for the absurd, and an elastic cast of mind.

However, if you insulate yourself at American-style hotels, eat at synthetic burger joints and quaff insipid brews, you might as well stay home and save the airfare. Authenticity, the real thing, is not easily come by — and just as hard to define — but some portion of it can be experienced by the patient, open traveler willing to walk the extra mile. And one of the easiest ways to do it is by attending a small arts or food festival aimed mainly at locals and mingle with them.

A traveler in any age inevitably will hear that this or that place is not what it once was, having sold its soul, as if Paris or Rome or Vienna or Rio have been so corrupted and diminished that they are no longer worth the trouble. An understandable sentiment, perhaps, but also a delusion based on some gauzy memory of past grandeur, more often than not romanticized.

Obviously, no place is what it once was. Change is inexorable. It is true that tourism, particularly mass tourism, alters whatever place it touches, usually not for the better. Even ruins can be ruined, as anyone who has arrived amid a squadron of tourist buses at Chichen Itza or Pompeii can attest. And unrestrained commercialism can be a cancer.

Yet that doesn't mean there remains no compelling reason to see and experience a place. A city is not just its architecture or history or the sum total of its distinctive food and drink. Again, it's the people. It's the rewards of immersing one's self in that living, breathing culture, warts and all.

It would be disingenuous to claim that your chances of having an intensely personal connection with a place are improved by being in the midst of hundreds or thousands of others seeking the same experience. But it is just as mistaken to dismiss the delights of a shared encounter. I recall a Sunday afternoon by Lake Michigan, where it seemed the entirety of Chicago – millions strong – was transfixed by the same event in the same moment, a dazzling air show soaring above the city. Everyone in high spirits. Total strangers behaving like friends. A palpable camaraderie. It can be that way, too. You just have to be open to it.

Go forth.

Travel Stories
Prague on the Rise (2012)

PRAGUE — The shell craters stand out in low relief, small blemishes in the grand, dark edifice of this city's national museum.

They are a reminder of the grim times, when the Prague Spring protests of 1968 were quashed by Soviet Union tanks and blood painted the streets below.

Today, they seem relics of a distant era. Rivaling Paris and Venice as the most beautiful city of Europe, Prague, freed of Soviet shackles in 1990, has made a quantum leap to (relative) prosperity in little more than 20 years.

Although its lagging per capita income still prevents the nation from bearing the euro as its legal tender, and such opulent shopping signposts as Prada and Dior can be misleading, signs of vitality are apparent everywhere: in cafes, galleries, shops and along the serpentine sweep of the Vltava river, crossed by 18 elegant bridges.

Chief among them is the renowned Karluv Most (Charles Bridge), festooned with 30 striking statues that seem decorous on a sunny day and ominous on a dreary one. Erected in 1357, it was the city's only bridge for five centuries.

All in all, the tableau would win the approval of Prague's most famous literary son, Franz Kafka, though he'd likely be appalled at the invasions of tourist hordes, not to mention the infections of Starbucks, McDonald's, Burger King, KFC and, yes, even Hooters, that compete with the graceful Old World architecture that is the city's trademark.

The beaten path

Tourists have showered Prague with cash, helping restore the glory of its heyday as, variously, capital of the Holy Roman Empire and centerpiece of the Habsburg dynasty. Not even 2002's extraordinary flood, the worst in 200 years, did much to slow the renovations.

This intensely romantic Central European metropolis of 1.3 million is now a polished gem, somehow blending a millennium's potpourri of architectural styles — Gothic, Baroque, Romanesque, Cubist, Art Nouveau, Renaissance — into a seamless panorama.

Where to begin? Wallenstein Palace? The Jewish Quarter (home to Europe's oldest still-open synagogue and the city's best jazz clubs)? St. Vitus Cathedral? The ornate Malá Strana (Little Quarter) and its Baroque St. Nicholas Church?

Most first-time visitors gravitate to the huge central square of Stare Mesto (Old Town), whose grandeur is breathtaking (even if it seems to have been conceived by Walt Disney). Nearby is the popular Black Light Theater, featuring an Asian-derived performance style enlivened by intricate illusion, mime and acrobatics, now a Prague specialty.

Just across the river, and offering a splendid overlook of the city, is Pražský hrad (Prague Castle), the world's largest ancient castle at seven football fields in size. It is here where the monarchs of Bohemia, Holy Roman Emperors and the presidents of the former Czechoslovakia and today's Czech Republic had their offices. The Czech Crown Jewels also reside here.

While such websites as www.prague.net provide useful suggestions, the most fortuitous approach to seeing the sights is to take a local walking tour or simply wander. Get pleasantly lost in the maze of Old Town's streets and you just may find yourself "transitioning" to Nove Mesto (New Town), which is not "new" at all, dating as it does to 1348.

It is this district that harbors a national landmark, the light-hearted U Fleku brewery and restaurant (11 Kremenocva), believed to be the world's first brewpub (1499). Even the oompah music is more charming than corny.

Though you won't find it at U Fleku, which serves its own dark elixir (Flekovsky Lezak), Czechs invented (1842) pilsner beer, and arguably the greatest of all lagers is the country's still-thriving Pilsner Urquell. The nation's No. 2 lager, Budweiser Budvar, was once locked in a long trademark dispute with American brewer Anheuser-Busch. But beer lovers worldwide know that Budweiser Budvar is to our familiar Bud what Dom Perignon is to Kool-Aid.

For those brews, try the much-favored literary tavern U Zlateho Tygra (17 Husova) in Old Town.

Czech cuisine is rather more varied than that of neighboring Germany, and if you had to pick one place in Prague to savor a meal, you could do much worse than Cafe Louvre (22 Narodni), across from the National Theater and sporting a fine view of the river.

Off the path

Offering a view every bit as impressive as Prague Castle, and a favorite spot for locals, is Vysehrad, another castle complex. Built in the 10th century on a hill overlooking the Vltava, situated within the fortress' high walls is the Basilica of St. Peter and St. Paul and the amazing Vysehrad cemetery, resting place of many luminaries from Czech history, among them Antonin Dvorak, Bedrich Smetana, Karel Capek and Alphonse Mucha.

Local legend holds that Vysehrad was the location of the original settlement that evolved into Prague, though it remains a legend.

Far more concrete is the city's (and the country's) tumultuous political and religious history, marked by the protracted Protestant-Catholic strife of the 30 Years War (1618-48) and, by contrast, Prague being one of the few European capitals undamaged by World War II (the Czech Resistance struck an agreement with the Germans).

The city's once large (120,000-plus) Jewish population was less fortunate, walled into a ghetto by Vatican fiat in the 1200s and later all but annihilated by the Nazis. Only an estimated 4,000 Jews remain in all of the Czech Republic today.

Not far from the city is Terezin, where one may tour the haunting Terezinstadt concentration camp, a sobering experience to say the least.

But Prague will not let you feel melancholy for long. It is a city vibrant and alive — inexpensive by the standards of most European capitals — with diversions aplenty and history around every corner.

A Flurry of Cherry Blossoms (2008)

KYOTO, Japan — It is an admirable and inviting capacity, to inhabit past and present so nimbly.

The city is open and international in character, not insular. Yet for all its diversity, its emblems of modern times, Kyoto is rich in ancient mysteries, still the Hana no Miyado (Flowering Capital) of old.

It is a mature but vibrant metropolis, feet planted firmly in the past, though with signposts of the present and future towering above classic machiya houses, two-story structures in which the heart of the city beats.

Kyoto, cultural soul of the nation, is the birthplace of many of the most familiar Japanese traditions: the tea ceremony, flower arrangement, sake brewing, Kabuki and Noh theaters, and more. Major schools of each of these disciplines were first developed here and continue to flourish.

Seventeen UNESCO World Heritage sites reside in Kyoto alone. Two thousand Shinto shrines and Buddhist temples lend their gravity, symbols and splendor. In all, 20 percent of the National Treasures of Japan are here, 15 percent of its Cultural Properties. It is an incomparable repository of the nation's artistic, religious and cultural heritage.

Japan's seventh-largest city with 1.5 million citizens, Kyoto lies, as Juliet Winters Carpenter wrote, "within the mountains as though held in a loving father's embrace." Surrounded on three sides by the Kitayama range of hills, the inland city rests in a basin, which makes for steamy summers. The streams that flow south from Kitayama converge in the Kamogawa (Kamo for short) and Takano rivers. It is along their banks that the profusion of cherry blossoms, so revered in this land, herald the spring, followed by a succession of other flowers in early summer through to a burnished autumn.

Though it smacks of hyperbole, one may circle the globe and not encounter a more courteous people, or a people more appreciative of one's efforts to adapt to and enjoy their customs and tastes. To be sure, there is an unmistakably Americanized quality to the high-rise hotels and office buildings, the mini-marts and upscale shopping districts, despite the pictographic language of the signs. But this rather unwelcome sense of familiarity dissipates quickly. Such signposts of Western influence and intrusion are consumed by the vast sweep of what makes urban Japan so singularly Japanese.

Golden statues glow in dark temples, the clip-clop of wooden geta sandals still echoes down narrow side streets, and immaculate restaurants seduce with irresistible aromas, serving as havens of tradition impermeable by time. Kyoto *is* Japan, a nation of 8 million deities that captivates a single inquisitive mortal.

A history in brief

Recorded Japanese history dates only from the late 6th century, and little is known of the country's evolution before that time. Kyoto's own history stretches back 1,200 years. Founded in the 8th century as Heian-Kyo (literally, Capital of Peace and Tranquility), and modeled after the Tang Chinese capital of Chang-an, a grid of long streets intersected by wide avenues, its name was altered to *Kyo* (residence of the emperors) *to* (city or metropolis), in the 11th century.

Kyoto assumed the mantle of capital from predecessors Nara (famed as the terminus of the Silk Road) and Nagaoka in 794, and remained the political center of Japan until the imperial government was restored and moved to Edo (modern Tokyo) in 1868, ending 265 years of dominance by the Tokugawa Shogunate and heralding Japan's emergence on the world stage.

That the ancient capitals of Kyoto and neighboring Nara survived World War II owes much to the efforts of then-U.S. Secretary of War Henry Stinson, who intervened to prevent the bombing of these cities and their cultural treasures.

Under the cherry tree

The Japanese tradition of hanami, or "flower viewing," has its origins in the Heian Period (794 to 1191), when it was popularized by the imperial court. Cherry-blossom viewing may be a national obsession throughout Japan from late March to mid-April, but Kyoto is arguably the exemplar of the annual pageant with its backdrop of strikingly beautiful temples and gardens.

The blossom of the ornamental cherry tree, or "sakura," is the national flower of Japan. Visitor or native, one does not merely enjoy the annual Cherry Blossom Festival here; you contemplate the trees' simplicity and grandeur. It's an annual pilgrimage, if only to one's backyard. The quiet explosion of cherry blossoms, in pale pinks or the dominant milky white, suggests renewal, but also a sense of the ephemeral quality of life.

Don't miss the Miyako Odori, or "Cherry Blossom Dance," held by the geisha at Gion Corner theater in the fascinating Gion district, the large area of central Kyoto east of the Kamo River. It is in Gion where one is most likely to encounter the graceful, magnificently garbed maiko, or geisha in training, who are every bit as irresistible to Japanese tourists with a camera as they are to Occidental travelers. Together with the Pontocho district, where maiko also glide through the streets, Gion is the city's chief entertainment district.

During daylight hours, the cascade of color that runs the length of the Philosopher's Path on the banks of the Kamo River is a prime viewing spot, as is bucolic Arashiyama Park (a short train ride away).

The Heian Shrine is famed for its unique "weeping" cherry-blossom trees, and at night, there are concerts held at the shrine featuring a dazzling light show. Adjacent to Yasaka Shrine is Maruyama Park, an ideal spot for sun-dappled or lantern-lit picnics under the cherry trees. But there are also numerous streets in Gion — flanking canals, winding narrowly into the night — whose cherry trees are illuminated from above and below, casting a magical spell.

Iconic attractions

Reputedly the first three-story building in Japan, the resplendent Golden Pavilion (Kinkaku-ji temple) is nestled in beautiful gardens by a pond at the foot of the Kitayama hills. The second and third stories are covered in gold leaf within and without. In contrast, the Imperial Palace is the embodiment of the Zen aesthetic of Wabi/Sabi (rusticity and elegance).

Much less ostentatious than the palaces of the West, it was the home of the Imperial family until 1868.

Nijo Castle was begun by the warlord Nobunaga Oda in 1568 and completed in 1603 by the great shogun Tokugawa Ieyasu (on whom "Shogun" novelist James Clavell modeled his iron ruler Toranaga). The main court of the castle was destroyed by fire in 1788. All that remains of the original complex is the Ninomanu Palace second court, but what a wonder it is, seeming more like an elaborate residence with its elegant gardens and a sumptuously appointed interior.

Dating from 1164 (rebuilt after a fire in 1249), Sanjusangendo is a Buddhist Temple famed for its phalanx of 1,001 human-sized Kannon, carved statues staggered in 10 rows surrounding the massive figure of the temple's main deity. Around the 124 original statues left untouched by fire stand 28 statues of guardian deities.

Fabled Kiyomizu Temple is one of Kyoto's most popular destinations — and most crowded during the city's many festivals — especially the massive Dancing Stage that provides a panoramic view of the city below.

As for the moss garden at the temple Saiho-ji and the gardens at Kasura Imperial Villa, visits must be arranged weeks or months in advance.

Getting there and around

The JR Haruka Limited express, or bullet train (shinkansen), departs every 30 minutes from Kansai Airport in Osaka en route to Kyoto. Osaka is your introduction to the colossal Osaka-Kobe-Kyoto metro area.

Your first sight at journey's end will be Kyoto Station, the futuristic railway nexus that resembles a space ark.

Central Kyoto is ridiculously easy to get around by subway, bus or taxi. Subway and bus stops are clearly marked in Japanese, Chinese and Korean, with stops and connections also announced in English. All bus stops have names. Taxis are plentiful, with the favored company known as MK Taxi. But you will want to spend a good deal of time on foot, especially in Gion. The center city's gridwork, a layout that is very rare in Japan, makes it a snap.

Consider investing at least one day in a guided tour of temples and shrines. Though you may feel a bit rushed, you can always go back to those that most capture your imagination and experience them at your own pace.

Where to stay, dine

Western-style hotels are numerous, but if you can afford the indulgence, reserve a room in a traditional ryokan, handsome inns that are the ultimate in Japanese hospitality. Some are important historical sites in themselves.

As a travel mecca, restaurants simple and first-rate are flecked throughout Kyoto, with a strong concentration in Gion. Kyo-ryori (Kyoto-style cooking) is marked by subtle flavoring and seasonal ingredients with an emphasis on vegetables. While you can spend a king's ransom, you also may dine like a royal and not break the bank. An extraordinary meal (of great culinary artistry) can be had for $40. Be sure to sample Kyo-kaiseki (or kaiseki-ryori), an array of artfully arranged small courses, often served in a lacquered box or tray of multiple compartments and garnished with leaves or miniature flowers to evoke the season or a poetic image.

You can lunch handsomely for as little as $10-$15. There's also the Nishiki market, brimming with fresh fish and local produce.

One main artery, Shijo-Dori, also leads to the fashionable shopping and dining area centered at Kawaramachi Station, where you should take in the malled avenue Teramachi-Dori and the basement of the Takashimaya department store. A shrine to sweets, it holds dizzying displays of colorful Kyo-gashi confections, a prime example of which is yatsuhashi, a folded triangle of dough with varied fillings.

When to go

Venture there in spring, late winter or the equally enchanting late fall. Summer is Lowcountry-like: hot and humid. Say sayonara to it. Why go halfway round the world to suffer more of the same when you can contemplate the cool in comfort?

CHAPTER 4

The Freedom of Traveling Solo

The Freedom of Traveling Solo

"I never found the companion that was so
companionable as solitude."
– Henry David Thoreau.

"Alone" and "lonely" need not be synonymous. Never confuse the serenity of solitude with the pangs of loneliness. Experienced solo travelers may get wistful now and again, seeing all those loving couples at candlelit tables or among the tides of passersby on city streets, but they also know the pleasures far exceed the drawbacks.

Solo travel can be amazingly liberating, even when it's more by necessity than design. If you open yourself, it can be a wellspring of personal growth. And, curiously enough, connection.

After all, as Wendell Berry has written, "Nobody can discover the world for somebody else. Only when we discover it for ourselves does it become common ground and a common bond and we cease to be alone."

Going it alone successfully is mainly a matter of approaching things intelligently, knowing your strengths and limitations, doing your homework and, above all, taking advantage of the flexibility this style of travel offers. Yes, the scourge of "single supplement" surcharges has not disappeared, which forces unaccompanied individuals to pay half again (or double) the going rate for the same trip. These extra costs sometimes can be prohibitive on excursions like guided package tours, cruises or photographic safaris.

Which is all the more reason to seek out those companies that have the single traveler's needs (and budget) in mind, or, with a little research, self-reliance and common sense, to craft a personalized itinerary and strike out on your own.

Traveling solo means not being distracted or deflected from observations and perceptions that are wholly your own, unalloyed — the lucidity of loneliness, as Paul Theroux puts it. When you travel solo, there are no compromises. You do or go precisely where you wish, when you wish, and generally have enhanced opportunities for meeting new people. And you simply will not believe how chance encounters, even fleeting ones, can brighten your day. Essayist Willard

Spiegelman likens random meetings to "four-minute swirls around a dance floor with different partners, little love affairs without consequences."

Strangers tend to give couples a wide berth, respecting the impenetrable "bubble" (real or imagined) in which they are encased, though admittedly, couples often have a better chance of striking up conversations with other couples. While it's simply easier to meet people traveling alone, one must still be circumspect. But don't be overly cautious lest you deny yourself some memorable encounters. Be receptive. Give others the benefit of the doubt. That includes fellow travelers, who can be a wonderful source of info as you explore.

Even when aided by a competent travel agent, solo venturing still means shouldering the responsibility for the success of your journey, which can be as empowering as it is challenging. There is also the question of safety, especially for women, though women alone have been indomitable travelers for a great many years, in all corners of the globe. A positive frame of mind, a willingness to explore, and an insatiable curiosity are vital. Remember that the most unlikely places can bear remarkable features of interest, be it the smallest town or village or a superficially unappealing sector of a city that harbors hidden surprises.

In fact, for all the wonders of the major cities of the world, investing time in a small city not only can be less expensive, but easier to manage in terms of getting around. Large cities can be a cosmopolitan hodgepodge, which is both good and potentially misleading; smaller ones embody a specific culture. Although for foreign travel it may be true that not speaking the language makes it harder to converse with the locals in rural areas, simply making an attempt to speak the native tongue usually is all that's needed to elicit a helpful response.

If a large city, make it a point to familiarize yourself with the various neighborhoods before going. Here is found the real character of a place, its day-to-day, ground-level identity and many of the most striking examples of architecture and inviting small parks, as well as affordable shops and restaurants.

A note on planning: Free-lancing it, leaving things open to serendipity, can pay off by presenting new avenues. But particularly if time is limited, careful advance planning (with a malleable itinerary) can prevent you spinning wheels and squandering valuable hours.

There is also the advantage of securing the aid of local travel guides, at least for part of your visit. This can be a real eye-opener, another way to maximize time and see those things most tailored to your interests. I found this particularly valuable in places like South Africa, when my journey was to cover a great deal of urban, park and wilderness ground. Do some networking or consider online resources like The Global Greeter Network (http://globalgreeternetwork.info), which has local greeters for hire in more than 100 destinations worldwide.

Of course, all this presupposes clear self-knowledge. It is instrumental. Will you be comfortable traveling alone? Will you genuinely enjoy it? If you are less certain on these scores, consider mixing things up a bit. Just because you arrived somewhere solo doesn't mean you have to spend the whole trip that way. There may be occasions when you'd prefer to share part of your time with a group, maybe obtaining access to places you can't get to unless accompanied by others.

For that there are special interest tours you can pick up midstream, be in hiking in Patagonia, a culinary class in Italy, hot air ballooning over French vineyards, historic walking tours or what have you. People with common interests and compatible sensibilities naturally tend to connect more readily.

Though it's still prudent to avoid the single supplement (double occupancy) charges, some reliable sources for group tour information are the websites for the United States Tour Operators Association (www.ustoa.com), and, for domestic travel, the National Tour Association (www.ntaonline.com). Don't overlook organizations and clubs, especially eco-oriented ones, that organize trips for their members, or groups like Habitat for Humanity International (www. habitat.org) where, if duration is not an overriding issue, you can sign up as a solo volunteer. Volunteer vacations in general can be a great way to go (as long as you're prepared to work). Check out such online sources as VolunteerMatch.org and GlobalVolunteers.org.

Bed-and-breakfast inns not only offer generally less expensive (and often superior) lodgings but always have been a wonderful way to meet other travelers and exchange information. Plus, the owners invariably have a lot of advice to offer. Hostels offer an even more economical alternative if one is hardy enough (or young enough) to overlook their sometimes spartan facilities. Consult Hostelling International (www.hihostels.com).

Many seasoned travelers swear by tours operated by Road Scholar (www. roadscholar.org). Previously known as Elderhostel, but having changed its name for obvious reasons, this respected organization offers learning vacations to more than 90 countries designed chiefly for the over-50 traveler. It isn't always cheap, and double occupancy rates are charged solos, but you can sidestep that by taking advantage of the group's roommate-matching service. A crap shoot, to be sure, but one that veteran Roadies say generally turns out well.

Personally, I find that conventional cruises on mega-ships hardly seem like traveling at all. Greatly preferred would be sail cruises in the tropics, say, or securing a cabin on one of the smaller (and admittedly more expensive) cruise ships that can go deeper into the fiords of Alaska than the big ships, affording the traveler vastly enhanced chances of seeing wildlife and other sights, not to mention more personal attention and better food.

That said, if you insist on going the conventional route, with its round-the-clock slate of activities in the company of hundreds or thousands of your close personal friends, by all means evade the double-occupancy trap by letting singles travel companies like SinglesCruise.com or SinglesTravelInternational.com assist you in finding a cabin mate.

Oh, and as for those "free" cruise promotions you get from time to time, when you start seeing fine print that has a litany of "port fees, non-commissionable fees, taxes, gratuities, transportation to and from port, a reservation processing fee, service charges, incidental expenses or seasonal upgrades, additional peak season charges and fees for booking 7 days either side of all State and Federal holidays," run for the hills.

The one surefire solo excursion remains hitting the road. For more on that, see the chapter *Glories of the Open Road.*

Lastly, though websites come and go, do a search for solo-travel blogs. Some are outstanding.

Travel Stories
Rambling in Barcelona (2006)

BARCELONA, Spain – Thirty years of democracy have not silenced echoes of the Francisco Franco era (1939-75), four dreary decades of dictatorship and a legacy with which Spain still grapples. Especially here in the stronghold of Catalan culture, a city with its own staunchly held identity, so often at odds with the homogenizing powers of Madrid and centuries of rulers.

Yet these ruminations on the dark days generally are reserved for the press. Rarely do they make it to the surface of Barcelona's teeming, colorful streets, save for the occasional riposte overheard in a café.

Since 1992, when the city wowed the world with its staging of the Olympic Games, the politics of the past have been swept out to the glistening blue Mediterranean, snatched by the wind. The chief debates one hears these days typically involve what to imbibe, where to dine or the best place to observe a human tide that waxes but never wanes.

On La Rambla, Barcelona's famous pedestrian avenue, a ceaseless promenade moves from dawn to dawn, its broad, tiled walkway flanked by rows of sidewalk cafés, newsstands, vendors and (literally) statuesque street performers.

It is the nexus of this sprawling city, gateway to the narrow Old World streets of the Barri Gotic and La Ribera districts and a straight shot culminating at a revitalized waterfront. It's also but a square (Placa de Catalunya) away from that other vital artery, the Passeig de Gracia, a lane in Spain that's mainly for the vain, given the corridors of designer apparel shops, high-end restaurants and Milan-like contempo-glitz.

Barcelona is a hybrid: fashionable and hip on the one hand, appealingly "ancient" on the other. As the focal point of the province of Catalunya – 6 million residents strong – it is the cultural, commercial and culinary hub of Spain. And none too modest about it.

Long the home of the Spanish avant-garde, its fortuitous geographic position and one-time mercantile dominance did much to establish an individualistic spirit that persists.

Apart from laughter, the most common sounds of Barcelona are those of the rest of urban Spain: A symphony of jackhammers in the morning, stereotypically rapid-fire speech, smoker's cough (accepted with cheerful resignation) and the cacophony of delighted visitors. The flavor is international, by turns exuberant and nonchalant. Catalan (a meld of Castilian Spanish and provincial French) vies with English, Italian, French, Swiss, German, Dutch, Russian and Turkish.

In fall or spring, the weather's magnificent.

On La Rambla

Eventually, all roads lead to La Rambla. It's like South Beach (Miami) with less humidity, richer architecture and (slightly) more clothes. Cars and compact trucks do creep down the two lanes that cordon the walkway, and mopeds dart in and out of traffic like dolphins riding a bow wave. But little impedes the walker from navigating on and off the promenade to explore the Museu d'Art Contemporani de Barcelona, open-air vegetable and meat markets, niche shops, graceful theaters and cozy restaurants, not to mention the pleasures of the old city next door.

Wander through the wrought-iron and glass-roofed Mercat de la Boqueria (aka Mercat de St. Josep), one of Europe's finest farmers' markets. Then stop to admire the renovated Gran Teatre del Liceu, Barcelona's most revered, and the first of the masterpieces of architect Antoni Gaudi (1852-1926), the Palau Guell, standing imperiously just a few steps down Carrer Nou de la Rambla.

Return to the main avenue and follow it to the terminus at the Monument a Colon, which heralds entry to the Port of Barcelona and the splendors of the waterfront, a lively venue for shopping, a sun-splashed lunch or nocturnal tete-a-tete near La Barceloneta (Little Barcelona), with its cutting-edge examples of modernist architecture.

Gothic quarter

Get thee back on La Rambla, heading away from the harbor. At No. 42, enter the covered passageway to your right to access the pricey but picturesque 19th-century Placa Reial, first stop for a tour of the Barri Gotic, or Gothic Quarter, Barcelona's oldest.

Depart the Placa Reial from its northeast corner (on Carrer del Vidre), cross the Carrer de Ferran and Carrer de la Boqueria and swerve right onto Carrer Portaferrissa, which opens into Placa Nova. From here, one enjoys a first glimpse of the Catedral (la Seu) on Carrer del Bisbe. Close by, on Carrer de Montjuic del Bisbe, is the Baroque church of Sant Felip Neri, and the fine Museu d'Historia de la Ciutat, off Carrer del Veguer at the 14th-century Placa del Rei. This city history museum displays Spanish, Jewish and Arab artifacts, as well as a cavernous underground section revealing Roman foundation walls, water channels and sculptures.

A few paces from the back of the Catedral at Placa de Sant Lu is the Museu Frederic Mares. Lodged in a Romanesque-Gothic royal palace, this admirable collection displays Spanish sculpture dating from pre-Roman times to the 19th century. Consider it a prelude to La Ribera.

La Ribera

No avenue in Barcelona, not even La Rambla, is so representative of its district as the atmospheric Carrer de Montcada in La Ribera, a maze of labyrinthine streets in which to get engagingly lost.

Just as Madrid cannot match Barcelona's gloss, neither can Barcelona quite equal the veritable history of art embodied by Madrid's triumvirate of the Prado, Reina Sofia, and Museo Thyssen-Bornemisza. That said, the coast city explodes with art, from its lively commercial galleries to the treasures of such temples as the Museu d'Historia de Catalunya, the Fundacio Joan Miro atop Montjuic ("Mount of the Jews," with a spellbinding panorama of the city at night), the various shrines to native son Antoni Tapies and Carrer de Montcada's own complement of the Museu Tectil i d'Indumentaria (a textile museum), Museu Barbier-Mueller (a superb pre-Columbian collection) and the Museu Picasso, among the most illuminating, if not the most famous, collections devoted to his work. In this country and in this city, to which Picasso's family moved in 1895, it's been a year-long celebration of the genius of an artist who never returned to his native land after the Spanish Civil War.

The museums are must-see landmarks of this residential quarter. But many other streets share Carrer de Montcada's sweep of galleries, stores and cafés. If, at night, some of the less-traveled streets resemble dark alleys down which you'd fear to tread, wait a moment. Soon you will see someone's granny waltz onto the pavement, unconcerned, and young mothers pushing strollers beneath pools of lamplight.

A good 'Eixample'

The upscale district of Eixample is a sophisticated mix of modern and classical, enhancing the Passeig de Gracia and its tributaries.

The primary attractions here, other than shopping and people-watching, are Gaudi's imposing Sagrada Familia cathedral — perpetually cocooned by cranes — and his fluid, glazed-tile dwellings: Casa Batllo, Casa Calvet, Casa Vicenc and the remarkable art nouveau creation of La Pedrera (a.k.a., Casa Mila), with its dramatic "courtyard" and inimitable sculptured chimneys.

A mile and a half west of Sagrada Familia at the foot of Mount Carmel is another Gaudi showpiece, Parc Guell, which served as a proving ground for some of Gaudi's organic approaches, seen in the park in the form of viaducts, fountains, benches and other structures.

Food and drink

Though Spain is noted for its excellent wines, especially reds (tinto) such as rioja, it was not (until recently) a temple to cuisine like neighboring France and Italy. Today, it richly rewards the adventurous appetite.

In Barcelona, the other city that never sleeps, eating is a relaxed proposition, as casual (or as refined) as you wish to make it. And at whatever time you wish to indulge.

Lunch often is the day's heartiest repast, customarily starting around 2 p.m. For simplicity's sake, and some savings, request the menu del dia (menu of the day), but know that the freshest ingredients generally come with featured items.

Tapas are the now-familiar appetizers that locals savor with beer or wine at the end of the workday or after an early evening paseo (stroll). Compared to the American variant, usually ordered at a bar or table from a bill of fare, tapas bars in Barcelona are more diverse and often cheaper. Many are arrayed cafeteria style, but you also can order from a menu. Tapas can hold you until dinner, at the civilized hour of 10 or 11 p.m., or they can be dinner. As with helpings of the real national dish, cured ham (jamon), take your tapas in robust raciones or smaller porciones.

Naturally, you must have the obligatory paella at least once, and the closer to the ocean the better.

Take your time. Exhale luxuriantly. Even at bustling outdoor cafés you are never rushed. The staff respects the fact that you are there to take in the people parade, to browse the paper or to share endearments with your amante (love interest). You don't even need to order food. Buy a beer, coffee, half bottle of wine, glass of water, and sit there for an hour, minimum.

Few "no smoking" signs are spied, save for museums and galleries. Ditto for catering to diets. Low fat? Low cholesterol? Low carbs? You must be joking. There are vegetarian bars, but they're like orphans who've wandered, unwanted, into a family reunion.

Night life? Clubs are flecked throughout the city, throbbing from 9 p.m. till you drop from exhaustion. Check out travelpuppy.com for the latest.

Put your personal prohibitions on hold for the nonce. Barcelona's too tantalizing to partake of half-heartedly. Think gusto.

If you go

The Guía del Ocio booklet, available from news agents and newsstands, provides information on cultural and other events throughout Barcelona, as well as contact details for ticket agencies. The free seasonal guide See Barcelona, which is available in hostels and hotels, also is helpful. The Palau de la Virrena on La Rambla has a cultural information desk, and kiosks throughout the city offer information on tour buses and their routes.

The Streets of Buenos Aires (2010)

BUENOS AIRES, Argentina – The history of this city is written in its telephone directory.

"Pompey Romanov, Emilio Rommel, Crespina D.Z. de Rose, Ladislao Radziwil, and Elizabeta Marta Callman de Rothschild – five names at random taken from among the R's – tell a story of exile, disillusion, and anxiety behind lace curtains," observed the late travel writer Bruce Chatwin.

Allowing for a measure of literary hyperbole, Chatwin was correct in viewing this sprawling, fascinating port city of 48 barrios (neighborhoods), oft referred to as a European city in South America, as one great "theatrical" staging ground. In his harsh yet penetrating essay, "The Return of Eva Peron," V.S. Naipaul expanded the comment to embrace the entire nation, calling it less a country than a venue for absurdist political upheavals. Again, an exaggeration, but one bearing a portion of truth.

Melodrama aside, Buenos Aires is, undeniably, a masala of influences.

Today, some critics moan that its singular character is being infiltrated by creeping Americanization, especially among the young. Yet for all it has absorbed from abroad and engendered within, Buenos Aires represented an economically and culturally insular society a generation or two ago.

For many, that has changed. For others, the rebirth may be less tangible. The fact is that many Argentines simply cannot afford to indulge in their own capital city's pleasures.

At night, from the air, this urban landscape of 13 million people (3 million in Buenos Aires proper) looks like a gigantic, illuminated circuit board, winking its feverish spectra. At ground level during the day, one is struck by the architectural styles – elegant to elaborate – of upscale districts such as Recoleta, and the contrast between the streets of Retiro or San Telmo (the city's oldest barrio) and the comparatively low-traffic residential enclaves of Palermo, Palermo Viejo (Old Palermo) and Villa Crespo (with its quiet streets and oak canopies) to the north. Each has its charms.

In some areas of the city, however, grinding poverty is just a few blocks removed from opulence. In this, Buenos Aires shares the same sad footprint as other metropoli. A classic example is La Boca, birthplace of the tango, a tattered though colorful working-class barrio originally settled by Italian immigrants. There is much to enjoy here, though it is one of the few districts that visitors are advised to depart before nightfall. The same advice holds, if somewhat less so, for the dockside areas of Puerto Madero.

For the most part, Buenos Aires' neighborhoods are remarkably, refreshingly green, from their innumerable tree-lined avenues and balcony cascades to Palermo's Jardin Botanico and adjacent Jardin Zoologico (Buenos Aires Zoo) on Avenida Las Heras.

Most tourist draws are within walking distance from one another or within short distance of public transportation.

Bustling, ambling

Recoleta beckons with posh international cachet, from the splendid centerpiece of the Alvear Palace Hotel (1891 Avenida Alvear) and famed century-old theater Teatro Colon (621 Libertad) to such museums as Malba and the exemplary Museo Nacional de Bellas Artes (1473 Avenidadel Liberador).

Here, too, are Recoleta Cemetery (where Eva Peron is entombed), the ritzier tango emporiums and shrines to conspicuous consumption, most notably the huge Patio Bullrich mall (think: Rodeo Drive in a box).

San Telmo, which just feels venerable, is a particularly rewarding barrio in which to wander, with somewhat less overt snob appeal and a heightened sense of history compared with Recoleta. A bohemian artists' quarter, it is the city's prime repository of cultural riches.

Accessed off Avenida Jorge Luis Borges (at Plaza Italia), the square at Serrano and Honduras in Palermo Viejo is a five-points confluence typical of the neighborhood's numerous public spaces, with flea markets, taverns, compact restaurants, boutiques and a funky, youthful vibe. The tone is decidedly relaxed, but not to say it lacks energy.

While some have derided the district for selling itself as a cheap playground for "well-to-do wastrels" from North America, the barrio's breezy appeal quickly subdues the cynical impulse, even if the boutique-and-bistro segment of Palermo Soho does seem more than a bit derivative.

Nearby is one of the finest steakhouses on the planet, La Cabrera (5099 Cabrera), whose folksy ambiance contrasts with its cross-town rival, the pricier, though impeccable La Cabana (1967 Rodriguez Pena) in Recoleta.

Speaking of steak, sampling (or rather, devouring) Argentina's famous beef is a must for all but the most confirmed vegetarian. But you will not have experienced the real Argentina without trying its simple, delectable empanadas. And by all means sip some mate, the country's traditional herbal tea. On such streets as the arching, barrio-spanning Ave. Santa Fe, café culture rules as the most civilized and pleasant way to decompress and take in the human promenade.

Dining out

Good deals on food can be found, but forget what you may have read about the currency crisis in Argentina, at least with relation to its effect on local restaurants. A few years ago, it was possible to spend $5 (U.S.) on breakfast, $7 on lunch and $10 on dinner with a decent glass of the nation's most seductive red wine, Malbec. No longer. Even the pizzerias sport prices all-too-familiar to Charleston diners.

Like any great city of the world, there are temples to haute cuisine. Yet if you want to experience the culinary soul – and more – of Buenos Aires, it resides in its bodegones, unassuming neighborhood restaurants of individual personality, modest trappings and good value that give "comfort food" the best possible name. Many began their lives as groceries. Some of the most favored, according to locals, are El Sanjuanino and El Cuartito in Recoleta, El Obrero in La Boca, Guido's Bar in Palermo, Pizzeria Guerin in the city center and Cafe Margot in Boedo.

The only things genuinely inexpensive in Buenos Aires are its squadrons of taxis. You don't need to take the subway to save pesos. Choose those cabs clearly marked "Radio Taxi/Remise" and venture all over the place for a pittance.

One fine guide to the pulse of the city is *The Buenos Aires Herald*, still the largest English-language newspaper on the continent. But you will find that if you make even the slightest effort to speak a few words of Spanish, most citizens (or porteños, as the locals call themselves), will be only too happy to try to accommodate you in English.

Do you tango?

Let's say it from the start. The tango is as overhyped a concept as moonlight, magnolias and Southern graciousness. That said, it's a dynamic art form that can be appreciated as a seasoned dancer, eager neophyte or spectator, and in your choice of fancy dinner theaters such as Retiro's expensive Tango Porteño (on Ave. 9 de Julio, allegedly the widest city street on Earth) or in more authentic local-color tango bars, milongas and dance halls, where all you need to pay for is a drink.

When to go

The Southern Hemisphere's seasons are reversed from ours. Summer runs December to February; fall is March to May; winter is June to August; and spring is September to November. Buenos Aires' climate is generally pleasant, with its changeable spring, humid summer, and mild fall closely resembling New York City's seasons. Winter temperatures are much like those of Los Angeles or Cape Town.

Buenos Aires has two airports: Ezeiza (EZE) for most international flights and Aeroparque Jorge (AEP) for domestic and regional travel. Give yourself plenty of time to get there from the city center. Taxis are far less pricey than deluxe buses. And the conversations are better.

CHAPTER 5

Adventure Travel (Bright and Dark)

Adventure Travel (Bright and Dark)

*"At sunrise, it's not necessary, or even desirable, to know
where you are going to be at sunset."*
– Dervla Murphy

I am a passionate advocate for nature and wilderness travel, with caveats, from a simple series of day hikes in rural England, swimming with dolphins in the Florida Keys or a camping trip on Michigan's Upper Peninsula to vastly more ambitious gambols like tackling the length of the Appalachian Trail or mounting Andean summits.

Done carefully, with a healthy respect for the wild and a knowledge of one's physical limitations, it can be the most restorative and inspiring of all forms of travel. Provided we do not, by sheer numbers, trample into dust what we wish to preserve. Witness the ever-increasing human pressure and impact on so many of the world's national parks.

Legions of travel companies and outfitters have emerged in the past 20 years to capitalize on the wilderness travel impulse, as well as some well-meaning organizations that seek to educate and edify as much as grow their businesses.

Just be certain you are fit enough to handle the rigors of the more demanding kinds of outdoor excursions. Within obvious limits, age isn't necessarily a factor, but stamina and endurance are. Can you manage 20 miles a day on the trail? Ten? Do you know how to comport yourself in bear country?

Just as important, do you understand your reasons for wanting to be in the wild?

It is well to remember that, for some, travel is as much escape (or even hiding out) as it is a re-creative act. Which brings us to the dark side of "adventure," especially the "heroic" kind embodied by many a famed explorer.

In some ways we are fortunate that the last great age of exploration, which is to say the early 20th century, is long past. It was an era of towering goals (like reaching the South Pole) and inadequate preparation, of extraordinary fortitude and astounding foolhardiness. We can celebrate its achievements and deplore its costs at the same time.

The men who embarked on these expeditions were hardy individuals, cut from a different cloth. They dreamed of being great no matter what the cost. But at some point we must ask where the admirable, and very human, spirit of adventure ends and denial of reality take place?

As Felipe Fernandez-Armesto demonstrates so convincingly in *Pathfinders: A Global History of Exploration* (2006), which goes back much farther, even those among us least skeptical of the motives behind the thirst for adventure may be persuaded that the real (or at least largely real) story of exploration is a cloudy soup. It is one composed of obstinacy, romantic delusion, fortitude, avarice, naivete, ruthless exploitation, willful stupidity, remarkable endurance, hypocrisy, credulousness, mendacity, breathtaking incompetence, profligacy with the lives of others and adrenalin addiction – a speculative venture at best.

The romantic quest for adventure, the race to be first, and the means of financing it, usually resulted in deflecting expeditions from their alleged scientific goals, assuming they had any to begin with. From science to showmanship, "discovery" degraded to a publicity stunt.

When were commercial dreams, arrogance or hegemony not driving elements in a millennia-long march of folly?

This is a thinking person's history, shorn of nationalistic twaddle and other nonsense. The author is clear-eyed, provocative (if somewhat cynical), rigorous in research, admiring and caustic in like measure. He delights in eviscerating hoary myth, and, at least as important as the rest, writes with a great deal of verve and quickening flashes of humor.

Of course, that's the short-term analysis. Long term, geographical and cultural discovery seems to have been a process of re-discovery: The epochs-old divergence of the species to the far corners of the planet and our gradual re-convergence that is the end product of exploration and rampant population growth. Somewhat oversimplified, but that's the gist of it.

Does this have me foreswearing all adventure? Hardly, though technology undermines some of the essential allure of it. Real adventure compels you, *forces* you, to see the world head-on, firsthand. The world not of your imagination, but the way it really is. Savor that reality, no matter how unsettling or stark.

But remember, however far you go, however remote your adventure, do as Chief Seattle advised us: "Take only memories, leave only footprints."

———————

Travel Stories
Manifest Wonders (2004)

PHALABORWA, South Africa – The leopard pads wraithlike across a narrow, rutted road, ignoring the vehicle stopped 50 feet away. A heartbeat later, one wonders if it was actually there at all. This most agile of the big cats is also the most furtive, rarely seen even by those who have lived in the bushveld for many years.

"You have no idea how fortunate you are to have seen one," says Jonathan Middleton, a professional hunter and guide with an encyclopedic command of the Northern Province's flora and fauna.

Fortunate indeed.

Here, on the periphery of Kruger National Park, one of the largest and oldest national parks in the world, there are a burgeoning number of private game retreats. And no electric fences, at least by the water's edge. Nothing between you and whatever decides to amble through your camp or past your rondavel, the comfortable thatched-roof huts common to the veld. A dawn hike along a river is more than a mere stroll; it is pregnant with possibility. Anything may emerge from the water, trot down from the thickets, drop from a baobab tree or cross the trail.

Middleton, who works for Mathaga Game Ranch owner Danie Malan, has seen them all. And he holds the same appreciation for the land and its creatures one encounters through so much of the region.

That the continent of Africa owns magnificent vistas and astonishingly varied wildlife is the planet's worst-kept secret, and the source of much romantic illusion as well as reality. Who has not harbored idylls of Kilimanjaro, of the Kalahari, of the Serengeti plain?

Or of South Africa's manifest wonders.

What movies and TV cannot communicate is how boundless it seems.

Most visitors to Kruger hunger to glimpse the Big Five: lion, cape buffalo, rhino, leopard and elephant. But with luck, one may see in a single day a stupefying array of animals, among them giraffe, crocodile, kudu, zebra, bushbok, antelope, hippo, waterbuck, hyena, African wild dog, baboon, impala, civet, terrapin, monitor lizard, springbok, tree monkeys, raptors and a bevy of exotic bird life that would make the Amazon green with envy. Just don't expect much actual green. This is bush country, and the principal shades this time of year (spring) are those of ochre and straw.

City Life

After the dauntingly long flight from the States to Cape Town — upward of 19 hours from the U.S. East Coast, including a brief layover in the Cape Verde Islands — those eager to get underway often venture directly to the north, near the borders of Botswana, Swaziland, Zimbabwe or Mozambique, or southeast, to the place where the Atlantic and Indian oceans mingle. But this is to miss another physical marvel: The dramatic, mountainous coast of Cape Town and environs. Make it your first stop, to decompress for a few days and gather your energies.

Nestled beneath imposing, 3,563-foot Table Mountain, with its rotating cable car and hiking trails, the city is one of the globe's most picturesque and cosmopolitan, with a temperate Mediterranean climate. When South America was ripped from Africa 130 millions year ago, wandering west to its present location, it left behind a breathtaking setting for human settlement.

Like any major metropolis, it has its problems, some of them unsettling. Many homes are gated, especially those of the prosperous. Guidebooks warn of crime, sometimes exaggerating its severity. Sometimes not. And few are prepared for the sight of the Cape Flats, an undulating shanty town built atop a bleak, sandy plain. Tens of thousands of impoverished Capetonians and jobless migrants reside here in hovels constructed of whatever is at hand, struggling to carve out a life.

Yet for all the lingering repercussions of its racially and politically charged past, not least the tension between the drives to recover one lost history (black South Africa) while preserving another history under siege (Afrikaaner), there is the sense that race is not such a flashpoint in a locale that is a sea of skin tones and languages (there are 11 official ones). This city of 2.86 million souls, like the country itself, is trying to get on with its business.

Some would like more of that business to be tourism. Europeans first stopped and recuperated here in the 1500s. Cape Town was founded in 1652 by the Dutch East India Trading Co. Europeans still come to South Africa's Mother City in droves, many drawn by prime seaside and mountain real estate at comparatively modest prices. Americans as a group have not been as much in evidence. This can, of course, work to a Yankee traveler's advantage.

Bed and breakfasts, like those ensconced above the city overlooking Table Bay, are the way to go for budget-minded visitors. The dollar-to-Rand ratio is generally attractive. And consider hiring a knowledgeable guide. What you may lose in serendipity, you more than gain in not spinning wheels.

The Sights

Apart from Table Mountain and its canyon-scarred flank, known locally as the Twelve Apostles, Cape Town's glories include the revitalized Victoria & Alfred Waterfront that is an intriguing meld of architectural impulses and styles, the spicy Malay Quarter, fine restaurants and proximity to the country's oldest, loveliest and deservedly renowned wine region, the Boland.

The region is just to the northeast of Cape Town, where the oak-shaded town of Stellenbosch, second oldest after Cape Town, is an exemplar of fine food and drink. Nearby, and of particular interest to Charlestonians, is the Huguenot Memorial Museum in Franschhoek.

Stretching out to the south of Cape Town en route to the high cliffs of Cape Point, one finds numerous bays and elevated outcroppings of rock that offer spectacular, restorative views. It is not at all uncommon to spy southern right whales cavorting near the surf. Don't join them without a wetsuit; an Antarctic current renders this part of the South Atlantic two degrees short of frigid. There's also that matter of great white sharks, the surfer's ominous companion, who are fond of the place as well.

Highly amusing are the colonies of jackass penguins blithely waddling about at Boulders Coastal Park. Less so are Cape Point's cantankerous baboons.

If you arrive on the cusp of September, the first days of spring paint the landscape with a palette of wildflowers that makes an alpine meadow look anemic by comparison. From minute blossoms embedded in damp moss to sturdy six-foot-high varieties on mountain slopes to carpets of wild lilies near the beach, the sheer array captivates the eye. Table Mountain alone bears 1,400 species of plants, more than many nations.

The canvas extends to the north, though more muted. There, the most arresting flora are the unique, often massive baobab trees, the succulent-like euphorbias, the ubiquitous impala lilies and vivid coral trees.

Kruger and the Drakensberg

Although some opt for the lush subtropical coast of KwaZulu/Natal, far more descend upon the vast wilderness to the northeast. The Klein ("small") Drakensberg Range, where the highveld culminates, is not to be confused with the larger Drakensberg Range in KwaZulu/Natal. Eerily reminiscent of parts of Colorado, this impressive escarpment on the South Africa-Lesotho border is a magnet for climbers and hikers. Its crown jewel is Blyde River Canyon Nature

Reserve. The canyon itself is the third longest in the world, running some 19 miles.

Dominating the hot, dry eastern lowveld, and one of the great wildlife-viewing venues on Earth, is Kruger National Park. It's a two-hour flight from Cape Town to the park portals of Phalaborwa or Hoedspruit. Alternately, you can drive directly on the N4 from Johannesburg and use your own car to ply Kruger's byways. Those with more time might want to indulge in the romance of a train.

Originally established as the Sabie Game Reserve by Paul Kruger in 1898, the park has expanded immensely over the years. It stretches some 217 miles in length and averages 37 miles in width. As awe-inspiring as Kruger can be for a first-timer – it boasts southern Africa's widest variety of wild animals – it is well to remember that the park does not offer a genuine wilderness experience in the strict sense. It is too well laid-out and organized, albeit unobtrusively, cut through with narrow roads and dotted with protected camps. Not that the place is tame, mind you. Leave your car or open game-drive vehicle (especially at night), and you risk being dinner.

But the very fact that it is so well-planned guarantees that one will see the maximum of critters.

Summer in Kruger's lowveld is oppressive, even blistering, the air thick with mosquitoes and the threat of malaria. The end of winter/beginning of spring (September) may prove the best all-round time to go, with average high-low temperatures of 65-49. But be aware that it is the rainy season. Peak time is from Christmas to mid-January.

It is best to book well in advance to get a rondavel at one of Kruger Park's family-friendly camps, analogous to accommodations and features to many of America's national parks, though typically with better food. Try the wildebeast biltong (jerky) for a culinary revelation and peri peri sauce for a salvo of the searing. But unless you are staying in a private camp (or are on safari), reserve your sampling of the country's main dish delicacies – the delicious springbok, for one, and the excellent seafood – for urban adventuring.

Drink it in. Fulfill a childhood fantasy. It's *Africa.*

Patagonia: A Space Without Limits (2010)

EL CALAFATE, ARGENTINA – Four times the size of Manhattan, and still a pigmy.

Perito Moreno Glacier is but one small fragment of the world's third-largest ice field, excluding the polar caps, surpassed only by those of Alaska and Greenland. Five kilometers wide, and rising 165 feet above a milky blue lake, it is modest by glacial standards.

Standing amid the swells and minarets of this massive, mobile sheet of ice and snow, crampons securing one's boots to a precipitous ledge, it seems, rather, a limitless expanse, with vistas that go on forever.

When an immense shard of ice calves from the glacier's bow, collapsing thunderously into Lago Argentina, the awareness of being on a dynamic structure is brought home – with a shudder.

Together with the storied peak of Mount Fitz Roy (a.k.a., El Chalten, or "smoking mountain"), and its accompanying range, whose jagged crests suggest a stegosaurus' spine, Perito Moreno is the showpiece of Parque Nacionale de los Glaciares, and a crown jewel of Patagonia.

Here, in the offseason of autumn, it is possible to believe that the region remains one of the last "edge" destinations for adventurers, undiscovered by the tourist multitudes. Not so, of course. Small pockets of Patagonia are experiencing a development boom to accommodate visitors. But wilderness endures.

'Ha! Patagon!'

"The story goes that Magellan cried 'Ha! Patagon!' (upon seeing a Tehuelche Indian dancing on the shore of San Julian in 1520), meaning 'Big Foot' for the size of his moccasins, and this origin for the word 'Patagonia' is usually accepted without question," wrote the late Bruce Chatwin.

His seminal travel book *In Patagonia* alerted the world to its glories and contradictions. Chatwin promptly debunked the tale, offering various alternative, if inconclusive, origins. None entirely satisfy.

Defined as a vast wind-raked wilderness south of the Rio Colorado, inhabiting Argentina and Chile, Patagonia ranges from arid desert to steppe (grassland plains) to towering pinnacles of ice. Apart from Antarctica, it is the planet's most southerly landmass. Roughly half again the size of Texas, geologists think its physical similarity to New Zealand is explained by the likelihood that they were once attached (before the epochs of great continental drift).

Patagonia is the land that lured famous fugitives Butch Cassidy and the Sundance Kid; set Charles Darwin upon his path of discovery; attracted visionaries, exiles and hucksters of every stripe; made fortunes for sheep ranchers (whose estancias are now mostly abandoned); and saw the establishment of the world's southernmost city, Ushuaia, in Tierra del Fuego.

The myths surrounding the fabled gaucho culture of Patagonia developed at approximately the same time as our own Wild West/cowboy myth. It is just as colorful and, often, just as apocryphal.

Los Glaciares

On the ice, history takes a back seat to living in the moment. Viewing platforms and easy trails at one of the main park facilities make for panoramic observation of Perito Moreno Glacier. The most dramatic views are to be had just above the lowest gallery, to the left, but there is no substitute for a "mini-trek" upon the glacier itself, the staging area for which is reached via tour boat.

En route, the sculpted forms of icebergs framed by a jagged mountain backdrop (on a clear day) vividly herald what is to come. Once on the crunchy, granular surface of the glacier, it's "whipped cream" peaks, enormous "boulders," deep blue crevasses and pale "ponds" deflect a sense of how this gradually retreating construct really acts: like a liquid.

The astonishment is that glaciers can even exist here, in a relatively temperate clime mere hundreds of feet above sea level. But they do.

Parque Nacionale de los Glaciares, established in 1937 and a good deal larger than its North American namesake in Montana, has an equally impressive sister park in Chilean Patagonia, Torres del Paine, which owns the same majestic monoliths of granite-like diorite, huge glacially fed lakes and burgeoning tourist trade, complete with eco-lodges and "rustic" luxury resorts for the well-to-do.

But getting away from the build-up and into the Austral Andes is a breeze. North of El Calafate, Parque Nacionale (a mere 40 miles from the Pacific coast) sports an inspiring network of hiking trails at both Lago Viedma — with its own stunning glacier and ice caves — and, especially, those beginning on the outskirts of the village of El Chalten.

A real dazzler begins just behind the National Park Visitor Center: Loma del Pliegue is a 12-mile round trip with a gain of 3,000 feet, plus 3 miles more and an additional 1,000 feet if you venture to the top of the third hill with the best views.

If you are uncommonly lucky, the banks of clouds that ordinarily envelop and obscure the spires of Cerro (Mount) Fitz Roy and Cerro Torre will part to reveal as impressive tableau as any to be seen in the Rockies or Alps. Trails leading to Laguna de los Tres (Lake of the Three), Laguna Torre and Laguna Capri (a superb introductory hike) are other possibilities. Park rangers offer up-to-the-minute advice on which trails are most passable and which may be too hazardous from snow and ice.

For climbers, Fitz Roy, named for 19th-century mariner Robert FitzRoy, skipper of the HMS Beagle, remains the most challenging peak of the Andean cordillera (a mountain range or "cord"). But many of its neighboring spires have yet to be scaled, a reassuring thought, as is the realization that much of this land, for all its long and often bizarre history, persists as virgin territory.

Wildlife is diverse. Most commonly spied along the waters, as they flow from glacier to lake to river to sea, are guanaco (a llama-like camelid), condors, eagles, flamingos, silver macaes, black neck swans, the Austral parakeet (cachana) and Magellanic woodpecker.

Autumn foliage covers the spectrum from golden alamo to the flaming red of Notro bush.

Gateway

One of several small, modern Argentine cities supporting the tourist trade, El Calafate may seem very like a South American version of Lake Tahoe, the California side anyway. Campers and backpackers notwithstanding, some of its creature comforts are welcome after a long day's trek.

And wherever in Patagonia one might be, wilderness is at your doorstep. In El Calafate, one of the larger communities of the province of Santa Cruz, it can be gained a few blocks from the main drag of Ave. Libertador, at Laguna Nimez. There, as dawn or dusk plays upon Lago Argentina, you can almost ignore the knowledge that an aggregate of hotels, hostels, inns, restaurants and shops (not to mention a casino) are at your back.

Different weather and light conditions alter Lago Argentina's mood, changing it from aquamarine to opal to lapis. When night swallows the sun, find a chair and simply gaze up at a crystalline sky. Stars blaze with an almost painful brilliance, despite the ambient lights of the town. Magnificent.

If you go

When to Go: High season in the Santa Cruz province is summer (our winter). It's warmer and more crowded. Others prefer the comparatively mild period from March to mid-April (their fall) as most tourist services are still open.

Patagonia's incessant, notoriously powerful winds have diminished, and the throngs have gone home. Meanwhile, the Patagonian beech forests have begun to wear their autumnal colors.

Information: Visit www.losglaciares.com and www.patagonia-arhentina.com.

CHAPTER 6

Glories of the Open Road

———

Glories of the Open Road

"Our battered suitcases were piled on the sidewalk again;
we had longer ways to go. But no matter, the road is life."
– Jack Kerouac in On the Road *(1958)*

You've seen the ads. A sporty car goes careening down a sun-splashed road, kicking up clouds of autumn leaves, nimbly negotiating hairpin turns, with nary another vehicle in sight. On most roads, even in the American West, the image is as preposterous as it is idyllic.

But it's not entirely a dream.

I discovered one such byway in a seemingly unlikely spot: the Upper Peninsula of Michigan, where on an average weekday afternoon in early spring I drove (or, for the biblically inclined, was cast out) from the vale of Paradise to Tahquamenon Falls and on to a lonely trail head parallel to Lake Superior — and saw precisely one car the whole way. The same for some 70 miles of road leaving Death Valley on the way to the High Sierras and, astonishingly, on a newly resurfaced mountain highway in South Carolina at the height of the fall foliage season, no less.

With a bit of luck, you *can* find such vacant roadways and, apart from the slightly spooky sensation of having the road to yourself, thoroughly enjoy the feeling of driving the way it should be: the gentle undulations of the road, a whisper of wind, the eager purr of the engine – that blissful rapport between man (or woman) and machine. There is also the insistent eroticism of American road signs: *Dangerous Curves, Soft Shoulders, Slippery When Wet* and the ever-popular *Yield*.

The rewards are great for those willing to take a (peripatetic) page from the late Charles Kuralt and go "on the road." Even in this age of stupefying traffic congestion, the open road is not an anachronism. You simply have to know where to look and have good timing.

But it's not just asphalt and vistas hurtling by. It is a laboratory, a school, a way of accessing what one is seeing – provided you get out of the car now and again. The undeniable fact is that a motorist in a car, SUV, or truck sits in something of a sensory deprivation chamber, buffered from the world outside, even from the full scope of the scenery. You are blocked by the glass of your windshield, distracted by engine noise, music playing, phone ringing (heaven forbid), children clamoring, random thoughts and, of course, by the speed of the car.

Stopping for a moment to stretch one's legs, stroll the verge and take a photo or two may be pleasant enough, but it does not pierce that envelope of isolation. You are still at a psychological remove from nature, still in thrall to all the comfortable conveniences and accoutrements of modern life. Backpackers understand this well. They know that a few days in the wilderness, real wilderness, is a bridge between you and the natural world. Minus the distractions, your full attention is applied to the environment. Senses and instincts sharpen. You and the land, you and nature, are fundamentally indistinguishable, one from the other.

Still, it is the road that gets you there in the first place, and it would be churlish to ignore the finer moments behind the wheel. On the road you can "recreate" who you are, even if your way is that of the romantic.

One of the beauties of driving (when the surround is pleasant and not an onerous chore or painful duty) is the simple act of decompressing, of shedding the skin of stress. The road is balm and panacea, especially with the accompaniment of good music, a book on CD or, if traveling with a friend, stimulating conversation. As much as I write in this book about the virtues of traveling alone, being able to share the sights and sounds of a drive also has its rewards.

But you have to travel some distance to get the benefits. By definition, a road trip is a fairly lengthy undertaking — days, if not weeks, long. And keep in mind that hitting the road can be a surprising culinary sojourn as well.

There is a wealth of books and online guides to the great drives of the U.S., Canada and beyond, most of them offering suggestions for intriguing stops along the way, as well as alternative routes and side trips. Although *Readers' Digest* is not exactly known for the comprehensiveness of its publications, there is at least one singular exception, the incomparable motorists' guidebook *The Most Scenic Drives in America*, whose latest revised edition was released in 2012.

Its detailed survey of 120 great road trips is perhaps the most informative and reliable of all road books, handsomely illustrated and with useful tips on when to go, weather, and making the most of a drive. It's been my chief guide on more than 40 road trips and has never let me down.

The travel publisher Fodor's also offers its characteristically well done *Great American Drives of the West*, while its up-to-date website (www.fodors.com) suggests a number of fine road excursions throughout North America.

Of course, you can just wing it, taking whatever country roads or detours that suit your fancy. No schedules, no itineraries. William Least Heat Moon surely was onto something when he wrote, "The open road is a beckoning, a strangeness, a place where a man can lose himself." Yet it is also a place where the self can be found.

——————————

Travel Stories
Big Bend & West Texas (2015)

BIG BEND NATIONAL PARK, Texas — At first the landscape seems barren, with parched shrubs, an absence of color and only the occasional roadrunner for company.

Then you start to notice the subtle gradations in hue, the surprising geological formations, the song of the desert wind. By the time you set foot on your first hiking trail, the beauty of Big Bend National Park begins to be revealed. Yes, it is remote, one of the least visited of America's national parks, but that very isolation is part of its appeal, and its biological integrity.

Located 290 miles south of El Paso, the park is named for a U-shaped bend in the Rio Grande River that marks both its southern reach and the shared border with Mexico. Big Bend, a landscape so memorably evoked in the award-winning film "Boyhood," rests inside the immense, forbidding Chihuahuan Desert, dotted with prickly pear cactus, mesquite, sotol and agaves.

But above 4,000 feet desert plants yield to yuccas, grasses and pinyon/juniper forest. Higher still, ponderosa pine and big-tooth maple hold sway. The Chisos Mountains, apex of the park, are a nursery for more than 1,000 plant species, 450 species of birds, 78 of mammals and 66 of reptiles and amphibians.

It also is mountain lion and black bear country, with rattlesnakes, scorpions and tarantulas to further enliven things in the warmer months. The Chisos Basin, deep in the heart of the park, erupts with wildflowers in summer, and is the staging ground for some of the handsomest drives and hikes in the West.

Big Bend marks the northernmost and southernmost range of many plants and animals. The same holds for characteristically eastern and western species that meet here, making it among the most unusual of park lands, with various natural barriers also creating a wealth of microclimes.

Geologic grandeur

Though it all seems limitless, at 801,000 acres (1,250 square miles), Big Bend is only the nation's 15th largest national park. Its geologic grandeur may not possess the otherworldly drama of Utah's great triumvirate of parks — Zion, Canyonlands and Bryce Canyon — but it is impressive all the same. Decidedly so.

The entirety of Big Bend, and a great deal more, was once submerged under a vast inland sea, and preserved fossils and shells are often seen. Water erosion carved much of the present terrain, having worn away the upper layers to reveal igneous rock that lay far underground for millions of years.

Big Bend features three majestic limestone canyons, the most striking being Santa Elena Canyon. With three more outside the park to the west, one of the best scenic drives in America culminates near the hamlet of Presidio.

There are more than 100 miles of paved roads, 150 miles of dirt roads, roughly 200 miles of hiking trails, and endless opportunities for camping, backpacking, mountain biking, horseback riding, bird watching, wildlife observation or driving. Elevations range from 1,800 feet along the river to 7,832 feet on Emory Peak, highest of the Chisos Mountains. The Rio Grande borders the park for 118 miles, which means plenty of options for raft, canoe or kayak adventures as well.

Historic buildings and ancient artifacts are found throughout the park.

On the trail

Principal desert hikes include the Chimneys Trail, Mule Ears Spring Trail and Tuff Canyon, while the Lost Mine Trail and Window Trail are mountain jewels. Though brief, the Rio Grande Village Nature Trail gradually ascends a limestone hill to offer sunset panoramas of the Rio Grande, and the Chisos and Sierra del Carmen Mountains. Nearby is the very popular Boquillas Canyon Trail.

Of them all, the Lost Mine Trail is the showpiece, winding through pine forest with dazzling views of Casa Grande Peak, Juniper Canyon, Pine Canyon and Mexico's distant Sierra del Carmens.

Plan to spend at least a half day motoring down the Ross Maxwell Scenic Drive (Highway 118) on the west side of the park, along whose length are numerous river trails (Cattail Falls, the Burro Mesa Pour-off, etc.) en route to the terminus at Santa Elena Canyon. Here, amble along the short (two-mile), yet magnificent, Santa Elena Canyon Trail with its 1,500-foot walls soaring overhead.

Worthy side-trip

If traveling in the fall, consider a 110-mile detour on U.S. Highway 62/180 out of El Paso to another sadly neglected wilderness area, Guadalupe Mountains National Park, before making the long but engaging ride to Big Bend.

A unique riparian woodland ecosystem is the highlight of the park, with October prime time for autumn foliage. The big-tooth maples of Guadalupe's splendid (6.8-mile) McKittrick Canyon Trail cast harmonious red, yellow and copper colors, earning the canyon's reputation as the loveliest spot in Texas.

At this point you have an option. Drive one hour north on U.S. Hwy. 62/180 to stay in Carlsbad, N.M., and explore famed Carlsbad Caverns National Park the next day, or dip south for 250 miles to Big Bend. If the latter, head south out of Guadalupe on U.S. Highway 54, then take Texas Highway 10 east to Texas Highway 118 south, starting point for the must-see Davis Mountains Scenic Loop.

Take the lengthier segment of the loop (where Hwy. 118 run into Texas Highway 166) to Fort Davis. Return to Hwy. 118 south until you get to Alpine (home to a fine craft brewery) and pick up U.S. Highway 90 east. Stay on Hwy. 90 till you reach Marathon, then follow U.S. Highway 385 south for the last leg to Big Bend.

Another of Big Bend's virtues is the clarity of its skies, far removed from light pollution. This stirring nightscape, among the best in the Western hemisphere, won Big Bend National Park designation as one of 10 International Dark Sky Parks.

The mountains are pleasant in summer, grand in the fall, with a rainy season in the desert extending from July through September.

Landscape art

Departing the park doesn't mean leaving the region's glories behind. The Rio Grande's scenic drive continues on Highway 170 west through Terlingua and Big Bend Ranch State Park on along the rollercoaster that is El Camino Real del Rio ("The River Drive"). The Fort Leaton State Historic Site also opens to views of the Rio Grande Valley.

At Presidio, pick up Highway 67 on your way back to El Paso, but stop in Marfa. A small town miles from anywhere, as is much of everything in West Texas, it is widely known for its offbeat installation art and for a world-class collection of minimalist works that reflect the surrounding landscape.

The Chinati Foundation (www.chinati.org) and its galleries were founded by artist Donald Judd, who arrived in 1971 and proceeded to put the town on the international art map. Its guided tours are lengthy and a bit pricey, but worthwhile.

Marfa also boasts some excellent, unpretentious restaurants, among them Maiya's and Future Shark.

After this ramble, you'll never regard West Texas in quite the same light again.

Park info

Big Bend headquarters are located at Panther Junction. The visitor information line is 432-477-2291.

Ranger-led activities vary by the week, and a schedule can be found at www.nps.gov/bibe.

Private adventure tour companies include the Far Flung Outdoor Center 800-839-7238 and Big Bend River Tours 800-545-4240.

Park-run lodging is available at the Chisos Mountain Lodge, which sports a full-service restaurant, gift shop and general store.

An Endless Coastline (2007)

MUNISING, MICH. – One state, 3,200 miles of shoreline, more than the entire Eastern seaboard of the United States from Maine to Miami.

Perched high above Pictured Rocks National Lakeshore, overlooking the vastness of Lake Superior, the waters of Michigan seem boundless. Here, on the sparsely populated Upper Peninsula (UP), where wolves and bears still tread, one need not look far for wilderness. It is all around.

On the dramatic arc of the Keweenaw Peninsula to the west or on the remote fastness of Isle Royale to the north, you stand upon some of the oldest rock on Earth, pre-Cambrian stone dated to 2.5 billion years. It is quiet in these forests of the UP. So quiet that the whoosh of its many waterfalls, the calls of birds, a whisper of wind through tall trees, sound like voices: "Linger here... you will be restored."

Positioned between the 41st and 48th parallels of latitude, Michigan is midway between the equator and the North Pole. The south is flat farmland. But the north, which for our purposes begins at Traverse City on Lake Michigan's Grand Traverse Bay, is a roller coaster of gently undulating roads. Heavily wooded, with ample lakeshore access and arresting views, it is also among America's greenest landscapes, rivaling Virginia's Shenandoah Valley and the Hoh Rain Forest of Washington State's Olympic Peninsula.

Four of the five Great Lakes define Michigan's boundaries. For the motorist, that's 40,000 square miles of Great Lakes vistas, with 83 harbors. The state also is veined with 37,000 square miles of rivers and streams, while glacial retreat left more than 11,000 inland lakes festooned with 3,000 islands (some with lakes of their own), many of them in the north.

Michigan's human history began roughly 11,000 years ago with the arrival of nomadic hunter-gatherers. Perhaps no state east of the Mississippi owns a richer body of American Indian history and lore, the most extensively chronicled being the Algonquin tribes – Ottawa, Chippewa (Ojibwa) and Potawatomi.

Volcanic eruptions deep below ancient seas enriched the Upper Peninsula – the "UP" to residents, who call themselves Yoopers – with a wealth of silver, gold, copper, iron, gypsum and dolomite ores, all of which were relentlessly mined, producing more wealth than the California and Alaskan gold rushes combined. Timber companies assured no first-growth forests would survive, but the forests have largely recovered since the days of unfettered logging.

Of dunes and tunnels

Traverse City, in the heart of cherry- and wine-growing country along Lake Michigan, is a fine place to start a trek. After an excursion along the picturesque Old Mission Peninsula, rolling agricultural land festooned with properties such as Chateau Chantal Winery (www.chateauchantal.com), head 25 miles west of town to the village of Empire. Nearby is the spectacular Sleeping Bear Dunes National Lakeshore.

Motor onto Pierce Stocking Scenic Drive, a steep 7.4-mile car route to a high bluff overlooking the dunes, some as high as 400 feet. North and South Manitou islands can be seen from this vantage point, 17 miles offshore. The drive also gives access to the demanding Dunes Trail and the moderately easy Cottonwood Trail, a windswept hike over the tops of the perched dunes.

Equally impressive, and even higher, views can be found at the terminus of the Empire Bluff Trail. Make your way back to Traverse City with a wine country ramble, driving the long but scenic Leelanau Peninsula.

From Traverse City north to Cross Village runs what may be Michigan's most beautiful drive, compared by some to England's Lake District.

Passing the towns of Charlevoix and Petoskey (with their many fine Victorian homes), the route takes a hard turn west at Conway and passes the resort community of Harbor Springs. Shortly after the entrance to Thorne Swift Nature Preserve, with its dunes and wetlands, you enter the famed Tunnel of Trees, a 30-mile archway of birch, maple and evergreens with springtime carpets of trillium blossoms.

Cars prohibited

Park your auto for the day (or weekend) and take the ferry service from either Mackinaw City (at the meeting of Lakes Michigan and Huron) or the UP town of St. Ignace — across the grand sweep of the Mackinaw Bridge — to Mackinac Island, a quaint (if touristy) historic site with miles of roads made for carriages and bikes. Once the biggest trading post in the New World, no motor vehicles of any kind are allowed on the island, assuring its unhurried, almost somnolent, character.

Even the massive Grand Hotel ("immortalized" in the drippy 1980 romantic film "Somewhere in Time") and its well-to-do clientele get their luxuries by cart.

In spring, you may have the paved "beltway" to yourself. Rent a bike and savor the solitude of a sojourn along the lake, as well as some of the sites along the way, like Skull Cave and Arch Rock.

Return by ferry to the Upper Peninsula.

Yooper heaven

The gem of the UP is Pictured Rocks on the southern shore of that greatest of the Great Lakes, Superior, the largest body of fresh water in the world. Yet even at 31,800 square miles, it is only the remnant of the once-gargantuan Lake Algonquin. The Rocks' 200-foot sandstone cliffs with their multi-hued faces — a cross-section of geologic time — are best seen from the water. Tour boats leave Munising's protected harbor throughout the day beginning in late May. Choose the last trip; sunset offers the most vivid panoramas.

Hiking trails can be accessed at a number of trail heads along Pictured Rocks' 40-mile-long expanse, running from Grand Marais to Munising. One path, the

Lakeshore-North Country Trail, travels the full length of the lakeshore. Among the best overlooks are Grand Sable Falls, Grand Sable Banks, Chapel Basin (great for day hiking), Au Sable Light Station and Miners' Castle.

But there's more to the UP than the main event. Start your trek in Paradise (the town), heading due north to lonely Whitefish Point on one of the chief raptor and aquatic bird migratory routes. Arrive in April and glimpse bald and golden eagles, northern goshawks, and Cooper's, red-tailed, sharp-shinned and broad-winged hawks. May brings herons, swans, loons and gulls, plus smaller birds of the forests.

If North Carolina's Outer Banks is the Graveyard of the Atlantic, this is the tomb of the Great Lakes, with a disproportionate share of the 6,000 ships lost on the Lakes, not least the ill-fated Edmund Fitzgerald. The Great Lakes Shipwreck Museum and the restored Whitefish Point Light Station are absolute musts.

Leaving Paradise (yes, even Adam and Eve had to), head southwest for 12 miles to Tahquamenon Falls State Park. Its Upper (more dramatic) and Lower (more tiered) Falls both are worth a visit, sporting some of the most tannic, tea-colored water you will see anywhere. The wide Upper Falls has been termed Little Niagara, and looks the part.

From here, one may head south to take in the vast Seney National Wildlife Refuge, go farther west to enter one segment of the huge Hiawatha National Forest, or head due north for Grand Marais and Pictured Rocks National Lakeshore.

At the western extremity of the UP are the Porcupine Mountains, the most extensive range in the Midwest. But that, like Isle Royale, is another story, as is the less-traveled south shore of the UP on Lake Michigan.

CHAPTER 7

Feeding the Mind and Spirit: Travel, History and the Arts

Feeding the Mind and Spirit: Travel, History and the Arts

"A mind that is stretched by a new experience can never go back to its old dimensions."
– variously attributed to Oliver Wendell Holmes

I am a confirmed museum and gallery crawler. It is one of my principal motivations to travel. Often, I'm surprised at just how many of these repositories of world culture, on five continents, I've been privileged to tour. And by how much — an immeasurable amount, really — I have gained.

To be transfixed by painting and sculpture, by the images of extraordinary photographers, the work of the great potters, wood and metalworkers, weavers and exemplars of all the enduring crafts is to be rewarded far beyond the effort required to find them.

Not to mention the brilliance of musicians, actors, poets, dancers and everyone engaged in that wonderful exercise of human talents collectively known as the arts. The great gardens of the world are no less an expression of creativity. As are our varied cuisines. Not precisely the arts, but certainly another way of feeding the mind and spirit are the many zoos, aquariums, planetariums and historical sites.

These touchstones enrich travel immeasurably. To absorb, and *be* absorbed; that's the crux of it.

If you are fortunate enough to live in a major American city such as Washington, D.C., Chicago, New York or Boston in the East, or Los Angeles and Seattle in the West, you can avail yourself of splendid little mini-vacations at leisure. For locals and visitors, what these metropoli offer in the arts is extraordinary.

Consider the Nation's Capital. Known internationally for the grandeur of its heritage icons — the U.S. Capitol, monuments, memorials and buildings on the National Register of Historic Places — Washington, D.C. is no less a mecca of the arts, boasting such treasures as the Smithsonian Institution's National Gallery of Art, Air & Space Museum, Museum of Natural History, the Freer Gallery, American

Art Museum and the Renwick Gallery, as well as temples like the National Art Gallery, Corcoran Gallery of Art and the Phillips Collection. Each beckon with their timeless, singularly impressive works.

One key to getting the most from the major museums is to go early or late, no later than one hour after doors open or one hour before they close. What you may lose in the volume of what you see will be more than offset by the ability to focus, really focus, on individual works without the distraction of so many other viewers. Go to less frequented sections. It will be a quieter, more centered and intimate experience, likely to reveal hidden treasures, brilliant artists who are wholly new to you. Solitary contemplation is your goal, not following in the flow of a noisy crowd. The approach is active, not passive, meditative and thoughtful. A universe unlocks its portals and invites you in. You are taken out of yourself in ways you never imagined possible.

This is the way to visit a museum of any kind. Or, for that matter, the great number of private art and photography galleries.

I confess that I have been guilty of racing through a museum, spending as little as a few moments observing each work of art, and obtaining only the most superficial experience of it. A dreadful mistake, that, even when it's simply indulging the all too human propensity to try to cram in as much as possible in the time that is available. It is all too easy to regard a museum or gallery like any other attraction: an entry in a log, one more stop on a checklist of world museums, a notch on a belt. What a waste. Don't do it. Given the time and inclination, you can always go back another day to take in what you missed the first time around.

Museums also are bastions of research and study. Name a scientific discipline, and there is a museum for it: archeology, anthropology, geology, mathematics, astronomy, ornithology, aeronautics, paleontology, natural history, pharmacology and more. Observing science at work can be as fascinating as watching a painter in her studio or a sculptor in his workshop.

Art is just the beginning. Then there are the symphonies, chamber orchestras, live theater, dance companies, jazz clubs, readings and audience participation venues. Or the marvelous acrobatics of such undefinable "dance" companies as Cirque du Soleil and Momix. You'd need several lifetimes to explore them all.

The same passion for the arts is found in Madrid, Tokyo, London, Morocco, Beijing, Mexico City and thousands of other places around the globe. Even the humblest small towns such as Marfa, Texas and Traverse City, Mich., are home to remarkable museums that rival those of major cities, while small cities like

Charleston, S.C., my home, can exhibit such renowned world-class emporia of the arts as the Spoleto Festival U.S.A., plus year-round festivals of the visual and performing arts.

Few things captivate the human eye and imagination like gardens. Some of the most dazzling are Keukenhoff Gardens in Lisse, the Netherlands; the gardens of the Golden Pavilion in Kyoto, Butchart Gardens on Vancouver Island; Dumbarton Oaks in Washington, D.C.; the Biltmore Estate in Asheville, N.C. and Middleton Place and Magnolia Gardens in Charleston. They are not only palettes of great beauty, but laboratories for botanical and horticultural experimentation.

Other renowned gardens, such as Brookgreen Gardens in South Carolina, Jardi D'Escultures in Barcelona and the Bestoff Garden in New Orleans are devoted to the flowering of sculpture as well as to that of polychromatic plants.

For all their discomfiting aspects, the best zoos like those in San Diego and Chicago provide breeding grounds for rare and endangered species, while helping succeeding generations understand the important ecological roles and interconnectedness of species.

Apart from the many historic districts of the great cities, and the imposing castles or fortresses of Europe, there are the shrines, cathedrals, temples, churches and synagogues, themselves great expressions of the architectural and fine arts. Even those not inclined toward religion will find much to admire at the St. Peter's Cathedral in Rome, Notre Dame in Paris, the Duomo in Florence, the Mezquita in Cordoba, Sagrada Familia in Barcelona, Tōdai-ji in Nara, Theatinerkirche St. Kajetan in Munich, St. Patrick's Cathedral in New York and so on.

Guided arts tours are available. For devotees of dance, classical music and opera, there are small group tours operated by such outfits as Travel for the Arts (www.travelforthearts.com), which operates 100 tours a year in such cities as Leipzig, Warsaw, Lisbon, Salzburg and Vienna through its parent company Specialised Travel Ltd. There are also à la carte arts itineraries for the independent traveler. Not only the famous venues but lesser-known theaters are showcased.

Also catering to small groups seeking a more hands-on experience are organizations like Arts & Cultural Travel (http://artsandculturaltravel.com), a "boutique" travel company that sponsors arts-oriented visits to Santa Fe, Taos, a Belize rainforest, private islands and now Havana.

"Life is short, art long," said Hippocrates, who knew something about living well. And great art thrives where there is a spirit of adventure: the artist's, and yours.

Travel Stories
A Cradle of Photography (2013)

*"Above all, life for a photographer cannot be a matter of
indifference. ... It is important to see what is invisible to others ..."*
– Robert Frank

NEW ORLEANS — There are many cradles of photography, no one locale owning title to its origins and growth as tool or art form.

Yet one may argue that this storied city, oft called the most foreign in America, is as central to the history and development of American photography as any in the land.

It has been said that, in company with literature, photography was the South's chief contribution to 20th-century art, having evolved from early portrait and landscape images to the unalloyed documentary approach of the Great Depression and on into Modernism.

Southern photography may claim some of the most renowned names in the field, among them E.J. Belloqc, Sally Mann, Ralph Eugene Meatyard, William Eggleston, Clarence John Laughlin, Birney Imes, William Christenberry and that darling of Southern letters, Eudora Welty, whose sensibilities were equally attuned to the power of the image.

"These and other photographers' influence on the medium extends beyond regional boundaries, affecting and influencing the themes, subject matter and aesthetic of the photographic arts worldwide," reads the legend from "Photography at NOMA," a recent exhibit at the New Orleans Museum of Art exploring the museum's 10,000-work collection.

And it is no less true of the photographers, like Laughlin, who found inspiration in The Big Easy or even called it home. While the legacy of photography in New Orleans is in many ways not representative of the South in general, one motif is shared: A palpable sense of place.

With images of New Orleans as its connecting thread, the exhibit, one of several notable collections on view at this time, features photographs from 1843 to the present, demonstrating the city's role in the history of photography through the work of such luminaries as Henri Cartier-Bresson, Edward Weston, Robert Mapplethorpe, William Fox Talbot, Andre Kertesz and Robert Frank, as well as by anonymous photographers.

Why New Orleans?

"I think there are certain things that did converge to make New Orleans an appealing place for photographers to be," says Russell Lord, curator of photographs at NOMA. "It has a strong and lasting architectural legacy. It's more than providing interesting architectural features to photograph; it becomes a backdrop for a way of life."

Light, climate, history, people. All contribute to the visual feast.

"I think the kind of architecture that exists here affects the way light filters into the city. I think the architecture forces people to move through the city in different ways," Lord says. "Then there's New Orleans' climate, its cultural heritage, its blend of ethnicity. This all creates a unique identity that makes it a place where strange things happen on a regular basis. And it's in a visual way, too, that strange things happen."

Certainly, there are other cities as attractive, as romantic. Paris or New York, for example, both of which command strong identification within our cultural imagination, Lord says. "But New Orleans, despite being so much smaller, has just as strong a presence in our imagination."

For some, the magic of "The City that Care Forgot" is best revealed in imagery.

Noted photographer and native son Joshua Mann Pailet founded A Gallery for Fine Photography here in 1973, establishing a venue to collect, showcase and sell 19th- and 20th-century pictures of artistic and documentary merit. His gallery on Chartres Street in the French Quarter is among the most distinctive and impressive one may find anywhere, housing original work by Cartier-Bresson, Ansel Adams, Diane Arbus, Yousuf Karsh, Helmut Newton, Edward Steichen, Josephine Sacabo, Fox Talbot, Alfred Stieglitz, Herman Leonard and many others.

"I'm growing very strongly in the belief that New Orleans has served as a cradle of photography," Pailet says. "Early on, when New Orleans was booming right before the Civil War, it had some of the first portrait studios in the country. It is remarkable all of the fine photographers who came through here, much like the many writers who came to the city."

And past connects to present.

"When you get to the 20th century, you realize what an inspiration New Orleans has been. Now it is reaching the point where people can step back and say this is a major hot spot of photography. There is something going on right now, and there is a continuum from the very beginning of photography here."

Pailet, born in New Orleans in 1950 and raised in Baton Rouge, has played an integral role in the support and promotion of photography for many years, producing as many as 10 special exhibitions a year at his own gallery while being intimately involved with other projects. It is a measure of his contributions, monetary and otherwise, that NOMA introduced its A. Charlotte Mann and Joshua Mann Pailet Gallery in November, honoring Pailet and his mother.

"I admire the way Russell Lord has curated his collection at the museum and helped bring this continuum to life at NOMA and the other institutions like mine," says Pailet, currently at work on several personal book projects, including a retrospective on his 40 years in the field in the U.S. and abroad.

"The creative community in New Orleans is in a renaissance and attracting very interesting people and events. It's like a fire has been lit under it. Photography is just vibrant, and I'm pleased to have a gallery that shows this contemporary vigor as well as the foundation of the classics."

300th anniversary

A second major project in which Pailet is engaged involves the observance of New Orleans's 300th anniversary in 2018. He's in the darkroom daily, busily editing and printing images he took of the city over that same 40-year span.

As a dealer, Pailet collects photography with one guiding principal: The work first must move *him*. "I've always been driven by knowing the history of the fine photography field," he says. "After that, it's by reacting to those images you see and fall in love with. Theme for me is a factor in my taste. I generally like documentary photography. But I also admire contemporary as well. Those tastes change and refine. I don't want something that has already been done."

There are more than 3,500 photos for sale at Pailet's gallery, not least his own, which grace the second floor. His work also has been displayed at such institutions as the Smithsonian, Library of Congress and the Polk Museum of Art, as well as being owned by private collectors.

"Everything here is for sale at any given time. When I sell a piece by a legend like Ansel Adams, I replace it. I like to anchor the gallery with the major masters, especially on the first floor."

Miraculously, Pailet's collection was spared the wrath of Hurricane Katrina in 2005, though he chose not to evacuate the Quarter, remaining to ride out the storm and document its initial impact and aftermath over the weeks that followed.

For its part, NOMA began collecting photographs seriously in the early

1970s when photography was not so commonplace on the walls of art museums. Today, it boasts one of the nation's most distinguished collections, handsomely augmenting its 40,000-object collections of French and American art, glass, Central American, African and Japanese works, and extensive outdoor sculpture garden.

"Photography at NOMA" is an arresting visual chronicle.

"New Orleans did become a place where photographers, even from abroad, felt compelled to visit," says Lord. "One other key component that can be underestimated is that there aren't that many cities in the U.S. where photography arrived almost immediately after its invention. New Orleans was one of those places. Photography was known of here as early as 1839, along with New York, Philadelphia and Boston.

"And what all that meant was that from the very beginning, this community embraced photography, and whenever you have that kind of auspicious beginning, you tend to hold onto it. We embrace photography as part of our identity."

Lord says that because the city is so unique, photographers who hail from here don't often speak for the South, though works often appear in exhibitions broadly about the region.

"New Orleans has a palpable sense of history and a palpable sense of death," Lord adds. "It's a city that's very old — in American terms — and has sustained remnants of its architectural legacy. Because of that, a lot of New Orleans photography has a sense of that and a sense of the past.

"Death is a very visible presence in the city, the way that people use it as an occasion to think of joyous things and to regard the continuity of life. Here, death is just a part of life. The above-ground cemeteries are a constant reminder. Life in a lot of New Orleans has a surreal bent and a sense of nostalgia."

As any devotee will tell you, its photography also offers *lagniappe* ("a little extra"), every bit as evident a local custom as that little something extra you're served with a plate of food.

———————

Edified in Edinburgh (2017)

EDINBURGH, Scotland — If the legacy of a land can be distilled in a single place, there may be no finer narrative in word or artifact than the National Museum of Scotland.

With its vast, 20,000-object collection, a new modern wing and an aerie overlooking this storied capital city, it is endlessly fascinating even to the most jaded of museumgoers. In just a few paces on a single floor one makes the acquaintance of such Scottish luminaries as the remarkable Isobel Wylie Hutchison (1889-1982), an arctic adventurer, botanist, painter, poet, author, journalist and prodigious hiker who thought nothing of an 80-mile "stroll."

Her countryman, Thomas Telford (1757-1834), was one of the great engineers, stone masons and architects of the 19th century. In the Highlands alone, he was responsible for 1,200 miles of road, 1,100 bridges, 32 churches and the 60-mile-long Caledonia Canal, as well as harbors and tunnels throughout Great Britain. Given the sobriquet "Colossus of Roads," his influence spread as far as Canada and India.

Their stories are just the beginning of the museum and of Edinburgh.

Resting on the Firth of Forth's southern shore, Edinburgh is a hilly, comparatively compact metropolis distinguished by neoclassical buildings, lush gardens and some of the most changeable weather in Europe. There is history around every corner, with its medieval/Victorian Old Town and Georgian New Town joined as a UNESCO World Heritage Site.

In the United Kingdom, Edinburgh rivals London for its cultural and historical drawing power with such sites as its National Museum, Holyroodhouse Palace (Queen Elizabeth II's official Scottish residence), the churches of St. Giles, Canongate and Greyfriars, the Scottish National Gallery and, of course, the imposing edifice that is Edinburgh Castle.

Perched high above the city on Castle Rock, an extinct volcano whose crest is swept by powerful winds, the castle was a sometimes home of Scottish monarchs (they generally preferred the more opulent Holyroodhouse) and today houses both the country's crown jewels and its fabled Stone of Destiny, a literal touchstone used in the coronation of Scottish rulers since 1296. There is no better view of the city than from its ramparts.

The city's other principal "hills" are 800-foot-high Arthur's Seat, a sheltering peak in Holyrood Park, and Calton Hill, a panoramic vantage point festooned with memorials and monuments that helped give Edinburgh the nickname Athens of the North. The city has a reputation for honoring its writers, and David Hume and Robert Burns, among others, are entombed here. Trails up Arthur's Seat are accessible off Queen's Drive near Holyroodhouse Palace, which is located at the base of the Seat.

Ancient Age

Home to the Scottish Parliament and the ancestral seat of the country's monarchy, Edinburgh has been occupied since ancient times. The earliest known long-term settlers were an Iron Age tribe the Romans encountered in the first century A.D. and called the Votadini.

Over the centuries, Edinburgh's traditional industries were those of distilling (its coveted Scotch), brewing and, later, printing. But it never quite turned itself over to industry and manufacturing to the extent witnessed in Glasgow.

Today it has a population of just under 500,000 and is the UK's busiest financial center after London. It is also a center of learning with an enviable reputation for excellence in the sciences, engineering, medicine, law and literature. One of four major colleges in the city, the University of Edinburgh was founded in 1582.

Apart from its 16th-, 17th- and 18th-century historical buildings, Edinburgh is likewise renowned for the arts, not least the Fringe, said to be the world's largest annual international arts festival. Festival season begins in August as Edinburgh celebrates the annual Military Tattoo and the Edinburgh Festival, as well as the Fringe.

Old Town treasures

Edinburgh does not have a historic district. It is a historic district, with the pleasing green expanse of Princes Street Gardens separating New Town from Old. The grand sweep of Old Town's most famous street, the Royal Mile, descends from Castle Rock to the magnificent Holyroodhouse Palace where, among other things, one may pay one's respects in the living chamber of Mary, Queen of Scots.

Along this cobblestoned way, the city's centerpiece and main thoroughfare, visitors are met with bagpipers in full regalia and the usual tourist haunts and signposts, but one makes allowances when the goods on display are everything cashmere, Harris Tweeds and the finest whiskys (or whiskeys). In any case, the vibe is agreeably low-key despite the crowds, and there are inviting watering holes, fine restaurants, the Camera Obscura and other entertainments to enjoy.

The Royal Mile's architecture captures the essence of Old Town, but Edinburgh boasts a much wider distinction with more than 4,500 "listed buildings" (a designation akin to our National Register of Historic Places) within the city limits, a greater number than London's relative to area. By contrast, New

Town (which began development in 1767) is laid out in Enlightenment fashion, with broad tree-lined boulevards, parks, and rows of tall cut-stone town houses sporting bay windows and enclosed gardens.

Do take the time to visit the 70-acre Royal Botanic Garden, an oasis of serenity founded in 1670, whose grounds are punctuated by 10 glasshouses containing 3,000 exotic plants from around the world. Famous for its rhododendrons, it has been a major center for botanical study for 125 years. Also, stroll through the Woodland Garden's giant redwoods. There is a contemporary art gallery in the adjacent Inverleith House. Admission is free to all but the largest glasshouse.

On a beautiful day spent in its gardens, Edinburgh's temperate, maritime climate seems odd for a city so far to the north, on the same latitude as Moscow, no less. But it can change in an instant. The old quip, "If you don't like the weather, wait 10 minutes," may have been coined here. Bright sun and gentle breezes one minute, glowering cloud cover and drizzle the next.

Even storm days can have their appeal. As Russell Banks so aptly described it in his recent memoir *Voyager*, "The rain silvered the city, hardening the edges and soldering its seams and planes, giving to the cobbled streets the cool clarity of a high-resolution black-and-white photograph."

Getting around

There is no underground, alas, but taxis and buses (tour and city) are numerous and, for all its hills, Edinburgh is eminently walkable. Nothing is more than an hour's walk away. Isobel Hutchison would scarcely be warming up.

CHAPTER 8
Travel by Rail

Travel by Rail

*"Travel is at its most rewarding when it ceases to be about your reaching
a destination and becomes indistinguishable from living your life."*
– *Paul Theroux*

S aying it is a cliché, but I can't resist: *All aboard!*

We grew up with the romance of trains, fascinated by their kinetic power
and mystery, their steely embodiment of strength and endurance, the music of
the shrill whistle and chugging wheels and gouts of smoke. For Americans, they
symbolized the joining of a continent by tracks.

A caboose-load of books has been written celebrating train travel. Can you
think of a single one extolling planes?

As a kid, I begged my dad to take me to the rail station on Saturday mornings
so I could watch the freight and passenger trains arrive and depart, stopping
briefly before passing through on their way to distant places. It was a father-son
bonding moment, and more. I was imbued, desperately eager for my chance
to travel in so majestic and civilized a manner, to be the one peering out the
window as the miles fled by.

Almost as captivating to my young eyes were trains in the movies, among
the ways we know them best. Since the days of silent films, trains have provided
splendid backdrops and set pieces, as well as dynamic platforms for stunts, fights
and other forms of cinematic derring-do, not to mention romantic assignations,
chance encounters and intrigue. They've even been key components of the
narrative, not just conveyances for the characters but characters in themselves.

Some of the most memorable films ever made, from Buster Keaton's "The
General" (1927) to Arthur Hiller's "Silver Streak" (1976), showcase this most
nostalgic of all forms of transport.

Nobody understood the potential better than Alfred Hitchcock, who made
four movies propelled by locomotives: *The 39 Steps* (1933, the prototype for all
sophisticated action-comedies), *The Lady Vanishes* (1938), *Strangers on a Train*
(1951) and *North by Northwest* (1975), the last credited by 007 maestro Cubby

Broccoli as the stylistic inspiration for all the James Bond films of the '60s and '70s, especially *From Russia With Love* (1963).

Arguably the most unusual of all train films, based on a screenplay by the Japanese filmmaker Akira Kurosawa, was Andrei Konchalovsky's *Runaway Train* (1985), often referred to as history's only existential action movie.

At its best, the reality of train travel is not that far removed from the fantasies, though many who grew up in the decades after the 1970s have been denied tickets to the great eras of U.S. rails. Traversing the U.S. often in the 1950s, Ian Fleming celebrated such colorful lines as the "Delaware, Lackawanna & Western, Chesapeake & Ohio, Lehigh Valley, Seaboard Express, and the lilting Atchison, Topeka and Santa Fe – names that held all the romance of the American railroads." What we may lack in contemporary *frisson* we more than make up for in a rich history.

There was a time when American railroads were the envy of the world, made possible by the skill, sweat, and suffering of countless men, not to mention the visionary ruthlessness of the moguls. The next time you take an American train, consider that between 1890 and 1917 alone more than 200,000 workers on American railroads lost their lives on the job and that another two million were injured. Makes you more appreciative.

Though measurably improved in recent years, today's Amtrak is hardly the Orient Express. Not all Amtrak lines have the most desirable amenities, compared to European or Asian trains, but you can still enjoy the luxury of keeping to yourself if you wish, reading, writing, or gazing at the scenery for hours, socializing in a viewing or dining car when the spirit moves you. That's not always true abroad, as in parts of the less-developed world. Fares often match or beat airfares, but Amtrak's sleeping accommodations are not for the budget conscious. And some great journeys still exist, not least the magnificent Chicago-to-Seattle and Trans-Canada runs.

Modern rail travel attains its apex in the bullet trains of such countries as Spain and Japan, hurtling along at up to 300 kph without blurring the view. It's like riding on a cloud, though you may miss the gentle rocking motion and symphony of sound of a conventional loco. But whatever type of train you choose, the advantages are many. Unless you are in a great hurry to get from Point A to Point B, rail simply can be more practical and less annoying.

The convenience factor: Unlike airports, which generally are a long distance from their host cities, train stations tend to be centrally located in major metro areas (and in smaller cities as well), sometimes within walking distance of your hotel or B&B. Also unlike air terminals, security checkpoints and long lines are rare. You don't have to arrive hours in advance of your trip or endure plastic airline food. Bring your own if you like.

And while some trains make frequent stops, they tend to be brief. Notwithstanding inner-city routes, travel by bus can seem to take forever. In Europe particularly, where the great cities are not separated by vast distances, there's nothing quite like visiting them by train. It can be done economically with a Eurail pass.

Some have rightly criticized certain rail routes in the eastern U.S. for offering no scenery at all, unless you consider claustrophobic walls of trees and shrubs to be appealing. But out west, and certainly in Europe, this is seldom an issue. Big windows and viewing cars afford passengers a panoramic look at the passing terrain and cityscapes. To my mind, there is no better conveyance for observing the scene in an unhurried, contemplative fashion or, generally speaking, a more convivial set of fellow journeyers.

Even at night, the romance and the mystery endure. Moving through the countryside, one's gaze may fall on one house in the distance, a single lamp light betraying its position, and illuminating your evening. What dramas have unfolded there? What joys and tragedies? What is the story that house and its occupants would tell?

I genuinely love traveling by car, but at best you have to have one eye on the road as well as one on the scenery, lest you become part of that scenery. With trains, there's no divided attention.

Then there's the environmental angle. In the old days, coal and wood-burning trains were the worst polluters. The reverse is true today, with dramatically lower CO_2 emissions compared to planes and automobiles.

As with travel by boat, another civilized mode when it's by river barge or small cruiser, there are a goodly number of reputable travel companies – among them Beverly, Mass.-based Unique Rail Journeys (www.UniqueRailJourneys. com) – offering diverse and attractive worldwide itineraries. Sift through them for the most reliable vendors and the best deals.

———————————

Travel Stories
On the rails to Munich (2012)

MUNICH—How are they doing in jolly old Munchen, land of the Glockenspiel, bratwurst and Bavarian cheer?

While the city's rowdy bonhomme does suggest a movie in which you find yourself an actor, just a few moments bending your elbow inside the Hofbrauhaus or outside at the Augustiner Keller beer garden may have you in the spirit, quaffing a dunkel or doppelbock and singing just as boisterously as the townsfolk.

Suffice it to say that, based on a four-day sampling of the urban mood, the people are upbeat, crime is at a low ebb, foreigners are courted, and all the taxis are pale yellow Mercedes (and all the taxis are new).

Munich, a surging economic engine, is Germany's third largest city, and arguably its most fun-loving. Like most European capitals, the most enjoyable way to arrive here is by train, savoring the splendors of the countryside.

Get your bearings

Though the tourist-averse may say Marienplatz is the one place to avoid, pay no heed. Start your explorations in this spacious city center square for the simple reason that it is still the best place to plot a course.

The square is a pleasant 10-minute walk from the Hauptbahnhof train station along the pedestrian malls that are the Neuhauserstrasse and Kaufingerstrasse shopping gantlet. Marienplatz also is home to the Old and New City Hall. More importantly, it's the nexus of the U-Bahn and S-Bahn base stations, as well as the launching pad for Mike's Bike Tours (www.mikesbiketours.com), Munich's best.

Spend at least part of a late morning or early afternoon atop Cafe Glockenspiel at 28 Marienplatz, taking in the view of St. Peter's Church and the unfolding city.

Don't be fooled by the wonderful "old" architecture spread out before you, appealing though it is. Large swaths of the historic district (the Alstadt) had to be rebuilt from scratch after the aerial bombardments of World War II, and much was re-created stone for stone in the traditional style. But this particular preservation instinct also lends the scene a vaguely theme park tenor.

Slightly incongruous in the heart of Munich, architecturally, are the three neoclassical temples flanking Konigsplatz — one containing a sculpture museum and another the State Collection of Antiquities — that together have been christened Athens-on-the-Isar.

Food and drink

The rather heavy, sometimes bland, nature of the general run of German food does not inspire hosannas, though like any great world city, a little research will render some gems.

It is, however, a paradise for beer fanciers who don't have to wait for Oktoberfest to quaff their fill or tour the Weihenstephan Brewery, the oldest brewery in the world.

While the cavernous Hofbrauhaus on Platzl is no longer reserved for those born to the purple and remains (like the Ratskeller) a quaint sort of dining and drinking interlude, a few steps away are the much less hectic and decidedly less corny neighborhood watering holes Augustiner am Platz and Augustiner Brau Munchen 1328.

Invoking the past

Tour guides are quick to remind visitors (albeit fleetingly) that Munich was the birthplace of the Nazi party and where the terrorist attacks of the 1972 Olympics took place.

A walk along the principal avenues radiating from Odeonsplatz is a bracing refresher course on how Munich and the rest of Germany were either seduced or silenced by the fervor of National Socialism.

Yes, the square also harbors the massive Kath Pfarramt St. Kajetan Theatinerkirche, a beautiful church whose confessional queue offers the comic touch of an automated traffic light. But you can't quite put the historical signposts of Nazism out of your mind.

By contrast, it is gratifying to see the black graphite monument to the White Rose Movement, a memorial to the Munich University students who resisted Nazi rule during the war. These students ran an anonymous leaflet campaign between 1942 and 1943 supporting active opposition to Hitler until the Gestapo infiltrated their operation and everyone was executed.

A different sort of arrogance and excess, of the royal variety, is reflected in the staggeringly opulent Nymphenburg Palace (at Schloss Nymphenburg) and Residenz (Max Josephplatz). The former was commissioned in 1664 as the playground for the son of Ferdinand Maria and Henriette Adelaide, then expanded into a palace that rivals the grandeur of Versailles.

The latter exhibits the astonishing wealth of the Wittelsbach dynasty, Bavaria's rulers for five centuries. Its 112 ornate rooms (in varying architectural styles) are jammed with priceless treasures.

Museum mecca

Of the trio of outstanding museums around Barerstrasse, perhaps the most impressive is the Pinakothek der Moderne, which displays one of the best Dali and Picasso collections in Europe, not to mention a fascinating modern design wing.

The Neue Pinakothek offers a winning collection from 19th-century masters, while the Alte (Old) Pinakothek showcases a slightly stodgier yet still interesting array of the finest German art from across the centuries.

Set on an island in the Eisbach River just three blocks from Baederplatz is the immense, extraordinary Deutsches Museum, a wonderland of science that pays as much attention to the technologies of weaving, glassblowing and photography as it does to maritime history, aviation and space exploration.

Oasis of serenity

For a more bucolic experience and a respite, there are the many pleasures of the English Garden, a huge central city park that dwarfs its Manhattan counterpart.

Here you will also find the totally unexpected: surfers. Munich is land locked, but a few witty German and American engineers, using a controlled inflow of the Eisbach River, had the happy idea of creating a perpetual wave "machine" in the northeast corner of the garden.

Wetsuited enthusiasts can be found riding the swells daily despite the "No Surfing" sign.

Up Leopoldstrasse, and far from the madding crowd, is the quiet district called Schwabing. It's a largely residential area once known as the Greenwich Village of Munich, but now superseded for bohemian trappings by the Westend and Glockenbach districts.

Still, it's refreshing to hear nary a word of English spoken, to blend in, and to sample less touristy restaurants.

———————

Forever Wild (2002)

LAKE PLACID, N.Y. – If you've seen one billion-year-old pile of rocks with imperishable vistas, you've seen them all, right? Not when doing the 'Dacks.

Mountains, forests, lake country. New York State's Adirondack Park is all of these. Summer brings a plague of black flies. But in autumn and spring, it is a hiker's and canoeist's nirvana, a journey through both geologic time and U.S. history.

Largely unexplored until the 1850s, the northern upper third of the state was besieged by loggers and miners soon after its wildness was breached. While it didn't stop the loggers, the state Legislature established a regional forest preserve in 1885 and the vast Adirondack Park in 1892. Two years later, all public lands within the park – the Adirondack Forest Preserve – were designated as "forever wild," never to be sold, leased or logged.

> *"Autumn does not sweep into the Adirondacks in a sudden onset as it does in New England with tartans of gold and red swarming in a single day. Autumn advances slowly, sending scouts and harbingers into the fading country of summer."*
> **– Lincoln Barnett**

Today, the park covers an area of 6.1 million acres, or 9,475 square miles. Grand Canyon, Glacier, Yosemite and Yellowstone national parks all would fit comfortably within its expanse. Though more than 50 percent of the park is privately owned, with 105 small towns and hamlets flecking the countryside, none even remotely exhibit the ghastly neon horrors of a Gatlinburg.

Some 42 mountains rise above 4,000 feet in the High Peaks region, the tallest being 5,344-foot Mount Marcy (from whose slopes the Hudson River originates). It is also the peak with the greatest number of approaches (four) for backpackers, though not necessarily the most desirable hike. That honor belongs, in the view of many, to Algonquin Peak.

The question is, how best to see it all.

Although there is no Amtrak train service that goes through the park, its Adirondack line still travels daily from New York City to Montreal through the attractive wine country of the Hudson Valley before skirting the western shore of Lake Champlain, where passengers can enjoy views of the Adirondack high peaks as well as the Green Mountains of Vermont.

Most of the trip on The Adirondack is scheduled during daylight hours, which is a major plus, and park interpreters board trains between Croton-Harmon and Westport, chronicling the region's history. Those planning to visit the park can transfer to bus service to Lake Placid from the regular stop at Westport (and to Lake George at Port Henry). Once there, you can rent a car to explore the park more fully, and later pick up the north or southbound train back in Westport.

Select a seat on the left-hand side of northbound trains for the best window onto Hudson River and Adirondack Mountains scenery. And since café cars on this Amtrak route can get a bit busy during dining hours, accompanied by high prices, it's a good idea to pack a boxed lunch or dinner before you go.

Others prefer to tour the park's top attractions entirely by car. Of greatest delight to road warriors and boaters are the 3,000 lakes of the park, many of them remarkably beautiful, and most connected by 31,000 miles of rivers and creeks. One of the more popular canoe routes follows the Fulton Chain of Lakes and Raquette River from Old Forge to Saranac Lake, a stretch requiring seven to 10 days to complete. At last count, the park contained more than 40 campgrounds harboring as many as 5,500 sites.

Though not as rich in wildlife as some parks, patient and savvy *voyageurs* will be rewarded with sightings. Black bear and moose are about, as are beaver, coyotes, river otters, deer and the rare bobcat, as well as herons and a variety of birds of prey.

Acid rain has taken its toll on some of the Adirondack's lakes and streams, but one will see no shortage of anglers, wading or in boats.

For an introductory glimpse of the ancient Adirondacks, take the 5.5-mile drive to the summit of Prospect Mountain, just west of Lake George off I-87. Take the U.S. 9 exit and enjoy a crest view overlooking the lake that Thomas Jefferson called America's most beautiful. Just try to ignore the less-than-stirring prospect of the *town* of Lake George.

From there head northwest on state Highway 28 to begin one of the nation's most picturesque drives, arriving first at Blue Mountain Lake, which inspired painters like Winslow Homer and Frederic Remington. For hikers, the short but steep Castle Rock Trail and the demanding four-mile Blue Mountain Trail, both overlooking the lake, are prime draws. Do not miss the justly famed Adirondack Museum, whose extensive galleries and exhibition halls harbor priceless collections of art, books, photographs and artifacts, and whose fine gardens open to a pretty view of the lake.

North on state Highway 30, pause to savor the settings of Long Lake (with its impressive array of birdlife) and Tupper Lake (featuring 40 miles of navigable water) before connecting with state Highway 3 east, which leads to the village of Saranac Lake and the Saranac Lakes nexus of water, trails and campsites. One of the better short hikes (a deceptively challenging two-miler) begins just outside of town at the trailhead for Baker Mountain, whose summit offers a spectacular panorama.

Mark Twain kept a summer retreat on Lower Saranac Lake for many years. Robert Louis Stevenson also lived in the vicinity for a time. It is easy to see why.

Lake Placid is perhaps the best staging area for attacking the celebrated High Peaks region. While less adventurous travelers might opt for the breathtaking toll road to the top of 4,867-foot-high Whiteface Mountain to the north, backpackers and day hikers will revel in tackling one of the great peaks on foot. There are at least a dozen peaks from which to choose in addition to Algonquin and Marcy – most with several different approaches and exceptionally well-maintained trails – but day hikers might prefer the splendid Mt. Jo, whose ratio of reward to expenditure of energy may be unmatched in the park. Reach it from the Adirondack Loj trailhead near Heart Lake.

Next, pick up state Highway 73 east out of Lake Placid and run the open road southward through the bucolic Keene Valley. The land falls away steeply from the High Peaks wilderness back down to I-87. Venture north on the interstate for a brief stint before veering off on state Highway 9N. Follow this due east to the town of Westport on the shores of the great inland sea that is Lake Champlain, with its sweeping valleys and echoes of the original inhabitants: the Iroquois and their arch-enemies, the Huron and Algonquin tribes.

Dovetailing with state Highway 22, the route heads north along a beautiful stretch of road which skirts the lake and seduces with such worthy stops as the impressive Ausable Chasm, marked by sheer, flora-festooned sandstone walls (climbing as high as 200 feet above the river) and the Willsboro Point peninsula.

At historic Plattsburgh, site of the American naval victory that effectively ended the War of 1812, you can take one of the lake's three round-trip ferry boat crossings to the Vermont side, then backtrack south, or complete the Champlain Loop by taking U.S. Highway 9 (or I-87) to state 9B at Rouses Point, just south of the Canadian border. There, connect with Vermont's Route 2 and travel south to the Alburg Peninsula and the Champlain Islands. Handsome state parks are positioned all along the route, which, on a clear day, afford views of the twin corridors: The Adirondacks to the west and Vermont's Green Mountains to the east.

Route 2 dead ends onto U.S. Highway 7 south. Stop for lunch in the terraced "college" town of Burlington, hub of one of the last areas of New England to be settled, then take a leisurely drive through the dairy fields, apple orchards and berry farms to Vermont Route 22A at Vergennes. Leave Route 22A for state Highway 17 at the town of Addison and sail over the arch of the Champlain Bridge, bidding adieu to the lake as the route crosses back into New York at Crown Point. Pick up New York routes 9N and 22 again, this time aiming south, and consider a side trip to the richly historic Fort Ticonderoga, the site (among other events) of Ethan Allen and Benedict Arnold's successful surprise attack on the British in 1775.

Resume course back into Adirondack Park and down the verdant state 9N along Lake George's western shore but reserve a few hours to hike the Deer Leap Trail, situated 12 miles north of Bolton Landing. It's the northernmost hiking trail along the peninsula of the Tongue Mountain Range, which pokes lasciviously into the mouth of the lake and serves up some of its more memorable views. Longer, tougher hikes can be navigated slightly to the south from the Tongue Mountain Loop trailhead.

Ramble completed. Or at least one possible trip.

Adirondack Park operates two visitor/interpretative centers that will mail free of charge a stack of indispensable hiking, waterway and lodging guides for trip planners prudent enough to do their homework in advance. Call (518) 582-2000.

Hikers anywhere in the park should be prepared for sudden changes in weather at higher elevations. While not the Rockies, neither is trekking the rugged 'Dacks a 100-yard stroll on a nature trail. Permits are required for backcountry hiking. And don't forget to sign in (and off) the trail registers.

Log onto GORP online and specify Adirondack Park for detailed guides to the best hikes. Ambitious hikers should make certain to carry the requisite gear and appropriate USGS maps, and ask advice of the Adirondack Mountain Club (www.adk.org).

CHAPTER 9
What Language Barrier?

What Language Barrier?

"The journey itself is my home."
– Matsuo Bashō

Anyone for whom English is their native language can travel with ease to all the outposts of the former British Empire and find those who speak our tongue: The U.S., Canada, Australia, New Zealand, South Africa, India and many a Caribbean or Indian Ocean island.

But it doesn't stop there. The fact is that native English speakers are a very fortunate group at this point in history, in that for so much of the world, English is — pardon the irony, Gaul — the *lingua franca* of the age, notwithstanding its great competitor, Español. Okay, so that's rather a parochial (and inexact) thing to say, and a billion Chinese speaking varied dialects might beg to differ. But it *feels* true.

Save for remote places, if tourism matters, English is spoken. In much of the world, English is understood (Paris being a notable, obstinate exception), which makes matters infinitely easier for the linguistically challenged traveler. Citizens of Lithuania, by contrast, cannot say the same, though they probably speak several languages anyway.

Now, if you do speak a second or even a third language, so much the better. It gives you a far superior chance of establishing a rapport, or at least a conversation, with someone in out-of-the-way places who does not speak English.

But let's say languages are not your strong suit, that you barely made it out of freshman Latin or sophomore French in high school, retaining little, and that repeated, forlorn attempts in adulthood to employ modern teaching aids have left something to be desired. In one way, you have an advantage over the multilingual when traveling abroad; you will not be overconfident.

To borrow a French phrase, you are on the *qui vive*, which is to say "on the alert" in unfamiliar surroundings. The very fact that you are at a loss, helpless before a linguistic obstacle course, means you must depend on the assistance of others. This may be slightly embarrassing. But as the essayist Willard Spiegelman suggests, it also means you are likely to be keenly aware of everyone and everything about you. Your senses are more acute, owing to an alloy of apprehension and curiosity. You see and process things in other lands you usually ignore (familiarity breeds obliviousness) at home. Sometimes, when the music of language is more important than the words, there is a kind of liberation. It is like the international argot of laughter. We connect with others despite the barrier of language, by relinquishing the language of sound and adopting the language of gesture.

All that said, it is no great trick to memorize a few key phrases in another language that will stay with you at least through the course of a few weeks of travel. More is better of course, but not generally necessary. It's the fact that you are making a sincere *effort* that really matters. People appreciate it. And you'll be surprised just how much those few useful phrases, combined with courtesy, will grease the wheels — and help you find the lavatory.

Of all the countries I have visited where English was not the native tongue, it was Japan where I felt most at home. Partly this is because in certain important (if not always admirable) aspects contemporary Japanese culture reflects that of America, and it's not just a passion for baseball. Like much of the U.S., Japan is highly industrialized, regimented and fast-paced (save for its ceremonies), with a high degree of urban congestion. As for getting around, 8 or 10 all-purpose phrases infused with a bit of politesse stood me in good stead.

Combined with a smile, they will do the same for you. In almost any language.

Travel Stories
In the footsteps of the ancients (2014)

ATHENS, Greece – It has become fashionable to disparage this sprawling city of 5 million souls as not worth more than a day or two of a traveler's time, as if all one might care to experience are the Acropolis, some moussaka, and a handful of centrally located museums.

The Greek capital is not an especially attractive metro area, the critics argue, despite a jeweler's setting of mountains and sea. So make your obligatory visit, absorb a bit of atmosphere, then jet off to the country's more esthetically pleasing venues: an Aegean island, say.

If you expect every city to have the visual splendor of Paris, the fairy tale quality of Prague, the style of Barcelona, then the argument is defensible. But not if you believe all great cities have their own historical, cultural and culinary glories and that making an effort to explore these treasures can be handsomely rewarded.

On high

Begin, of course, with the Acropolis, its unsurpassed architectural brilliance looming 200 feet above the city. And marvel at the fact that its structures have survived various, often incongruous, incarnations: Turkish harem, Florentine palace, Islamic mosque and ammo dump. The elegant Erechtheion temple restoration is complete, and conservation work continues on the Parthenon, the Temple of Athena Nike and the Propylaea.

If you're here in summer, make sure to go in the early morning. Otherwise, the sun is blinding and the heat blistering. Expect to invest a minimum of four hours discovering this iconic site, including a stop at the contrastingly modernist Acropolis Museum, which debuted in 2009.

But before passing through through Beulé Gate to take in the Acropolis' wonders, first survey it from the summit of nearby Filopappou Hill, accessed from the same Unification of Archaeological Sites promenade that skirts the Acropolis and leads to other key Archaeological Park historic sites like the Ancient Agora (marketplace), the Odeon of Herodes Atticus, and the Hephaisteion (460 B.C.), the best preserved temple in the city despite predating the Parthenon.

The tree-lined pedestrian walkway, which goes by the street name Dionyssiou Areopagitou, begins at the Acropolis Metro stop and culminates in the Thission district, flecked with appealing cafés and tavernas and offering one of the city's most beautiful vistas of the Acropolis.

Discover the districts

Athens' identity is a composite of its distinctive neighborhoods, from prosperous Kolonaki (which hugs the base of Athens highest point, 909-foot Mt. Lycabettus) to the nightlife meccas of Psiri, Keramikos, and the Gazi to the touristy but charming streets of the Plaka. Part of the Plaka, tucked into the northeast slope of the Acropolis, is the winding, narrow enclave of Anafiotika, whose chockablock white residences and floral effusions suggest an island neighborhood of the Cyclades more than Athens proper.

Go prepared. Maintained by a North Carolina resident with lengthy ties to Greece, "Matt Barrett's Athens Survival Guide" (www.athensguide.com) is the indispensable primer for the city, richly detailed and illustrated yet mercifully free of the typical guidebook and tourist bureau lily gilding. His guide is worth it for the district-by-district restaurant and night club recommendations alone.

Of the various "must-see" cityscapes he champions, high on the list is Athinas Street, sort of the real Athens in microcosm. Running from Omonia Square to Monastiraki Square, it intersects with Athens' top clothes shopping street, Ermou, in the Psiri district, home to the famous shop (on Ag Theklas St.) of Melissinos, the Poet and Sandal-Maker. A working-class enclave by day, at night Psiri transforms into a major café and club destination. But the main morning attraction along Athinas' length is the festival of color that is Athens' bustling Central Market. The busy street eventually deposits the stroller in the districts of Monastiraki, Thission and Gazi.

East and West

There's mild irony in the fact that Greece, the Cradle of Western Ways, is in eastern Europe, and several areas of Athens, especially the bazaar-like district of Monasteraki, has an Eastern look and feel.

Greece has been an independent country only since 1829. Like Italy, it shares the illusion of being an ancient country, when in fact that for most of the last 2,000 years neither owned genuine statehood. For 400 years, Greece was ruled by the Ottoman Turks.

Francis Tapon, author of *The Hidden Europe*, wonders if Greece "has a big strong ego or a small fragile one," a question amplified by the financial crisis that Athenians, battered by high unemployment, insist is subsiding. To be sure, Greeks sometimes seem almost inordinately proud of their country, with Athens as its epicenter, which smacks of living in the past. But given 3,500 years of history (twice that if you count the first settlement around 5,000 B.C.) and the profound cultural influence of classical Greece, one makes allowances.

If modern day Athenians, reveling in the glory days, feel at a loss to rival the achievements of Pericles, Aristotle, Sophocles and their kin, neither can Americans claim contemporary statesmen and Enlightenment-infused thinkers to match the Founding Fathers.

Museum mecca

Though the conservation/restoration impulse has not always been prevalent in Greek life, today's public and private museums of Athens are the equal of any in the world. A marvel by any reckoning, the National Archaeological Museum (28 Oktovriou St.), harbors a vast array of artifacts echoing the many millennia of Greek civilization, while smaller museums such as the Goulandris Museum of Cycladic Art (4 Neofitou Douka) and the Byzantine and Christian Museum (22 Vas. Sofias Ave.) showcase the histories of particular regions or periods with admirable felicity.

But the jewel in the crown may be the Benaki Museum (1 Koumbarei), located across from the National Gardens near Syntagma (Constitution) Square. Established in 1930 and housed in the one-time Benakis family mansion, the museum contains Greek works of art from prehistorical to modern times, as well as an extensive collection of Asian art. The Benakis family donated its collection of more than 37,000 Islamic and Byzantine objects in 1931, with another 9,000 artifacts added in the 1970s. Since that time, the collection has been expanded by some 60,000 objects, books and documents. During its grand re-opening in 2000, a series of satellite museums were created to focus on specific collections, allowing the main museum to focus on Greek culture.

The National Gallery of Art (50 Vasileos Konstantinou St.) presents permanent collections of Greek painting and sculpture of the 19th and 20th centuries as well as traveling exhibitions.

Also within the National Gardens are storied Hadrian's Arch and the remains of the massive Temple of the Olympian Zeus.

Expect something of a political history lesson at the Acropolis museum, where they still await the return of the Elgin Marbles. These prime segments of the frieze on the Parthenon, along with one of the Korai maidens from the Erechthion temple adjacent to it (and numerous other artifacts), were "sold" — stolen, as far as Athenians are concerned — to Lord Elgin of Great Britain during the Turkish occupation and have long resided in the British Museum. Greece wants them back, and has just the museum to protect them now.

For more history, ponder a day trip south by car or bus to gorgeous Cape Sounion, long a strategic outpost of the Athenian empire and home to the majestic ruin of the Temple of Poseidon. Alternately, head out beyond the city's southern fringes for Piraeus, a lively port city with fine waterside fish tavernas and Saronic Gulf views.

Language barrier?

Linguists tell us that 40 percent of the English language is French, that there are legions of Arabic loan words, and that another 12 percent of our vocabulary derives from Greek. But for visitors there's that inconvenient matter of the puzzling Greek (Cyrillic) alphabet, and such little quirks as that their word for "yes" ("ne") sounds like "nay," while "no" is expressed as "okhi" (which sounds like "okay" to English speakers). This is of no consequence, however, since almost all city street and business signs are in both alphabets. And you will be hard pressed to find an Athenian who doesn't speak serviceable English.

Getting around

The simplest way to get downtown from Eleftherios Venizelos International airport is the Metro, which costs about 8 euro and goes to Monastiraki after stops at all the principal stations in between. Just beware of pickpockets on this route; it's their chief hunting ground. The airport also is connected via the Proastiakos-Suburban Railway to Athens' central Larissis Station.

Central Athens is for strollers (*Peripatos,* in Greek), with many streets closed to cars and trucks (but not motorbikes). The city's other traffic-choked streets received major relief with the completion of the new Metro prior to the Olympic Games of 2004, and this clean, efficient system (some stations contain their own museums of artifacts uncovered on site) is among the simplest to use anywhere with just three main lines (Red, Blue, Green). For a breezy introduction to the city, and a way to get your bearings, consider taking the Athens City Sightseeing Bus ("Hop on, Hop Off Bus"), which stops at most of the city's central squares.

The Greek National Tourism Organization is situated at 7 Tsoha St. in the Ambelokipi district, while the Athens Welcome Center conducts daily, 90-minute historic tours of downtown and surrounding neighborhoods. You may also consult the city website www.breathtakingathens.com, the Athens Welcome Center (which operates daily historic tours of downtown and surrounding neighborhoods), and such English-language publications as *Odyssey,* the Greek daily news supplement *Kathimerini* inside the *International Herald-Tribune,* and the *New York Times* International Edition.

Pack light, but be sure to bring a robust appetite, an appreciation for the many crosscurrents of history, and a desire to immerse yourself in the embrace of a warm, demonstrative people who know how to live, even in the midst of crisis.

Lively, tolerant Amsterdam (2012)

AMSTERDAM — A traveler doesn't know where he's going, said the scribe; a tourist doesn't know where he's been.

A sneer plays about the lips of most travel writers when they utter the word "tourist," preferring to embrace the conceit that they and the like-minded are "travelers," distinct from the benighted category of visitor infamous for gaudy attire, clueless behavior and a lack of discernment.

But does the stereotype really hold?

This small, energetic and exceptionally tolerant city, though dense with tourists, welcomes them enthusiastically. And the reasons are not just economic. There is a sense of camaraderie here, of shared delight. The Dutch admire curiosity. And what but curiosity, a desire to explore the unfamiliar, compels someone to cross continents and oceans to take in the sights?

Take a moment to talk to the tourist next to you on the tram, the canal cruise, in the Van Gogh Museum, and rather than a boor or uncultured Philistine, you may discover someone far more worldly than you expect. After all, the "beaten track" of tourism becomes that for a reason. It's where the main points of interest reside.

One could argue that today's travel clichés are precisely the sort of off-the-beaten-track adventures where you are less likely to meet the locals, much less be welcomed into their lives.

Inviting atmosphere

Amsterdam has all the elements of an inviting urban experience: an appealing quality of life; a distinctive topography defined by its many canals; a remarkable history as the seat of a 17th-century maritime power; a rich, varied culture; fascinating architecture; and close proximity to some of the most stunning flower plantations and gardens in the world.

It is home of the first stock exchange and, for more than 400 years, the city also has been a center of the diamond trade. But less glittery pleasures take precedence.

Even were it not for the fast, efficient mass-transit system of trams, Metro and buses, Amsterdam would be an easy city to navigate. It's eminently walkable, and the concentric canals make it almost impossible to get lost (unless you wish to).

In addition to the Amstel River, Amsterdam — "Mokum" to locals — has one of the largest harbors in Europe, and most canal cruises also will usher you into the periphery of the shipping lanes. It doesn't take long before one realizes that the city shares at least one characteristic with New Orleans: At high tide, parts of Amsterdam are below sea level.

Pedestrians, have a care. Bikes rule in Amsterdam. So look both ways, or rent one yourself.

Dam Square, a few blocks north of the rail nexus of Central Station, may be the historical city center, home to the Royal Palace and whatnot. But before you flee into the neighborhoods along the canals to find the real city (and enjoy a little breathing room), beer lovers should treat themselves to one of the oldest taverns in Europe.

A mecca of the craft brewer's art, In De Wildeman is nestled inconspicuously on Kolksteeg, just off the shopping promenade of Nieuwendijh, and one of only 30 members of the beer tappers coalition of the Netherlands. Order a De Eeem Extreem, or any other of the day's eight to 10 specials, and marvel. It's splendor in the glass.

Cultural nexus

Three of the city's top cultural attractions are joined by the same plaza (Museum-Plein): the Van Gogh Museum, the (national) Rijksmuseum; and the famed concert hall Concertgebouw, with a fashionable commercial art and antiques district just to the north.

Also not to be missed: the Anne Frank House, a haunting, worthwhile experience despite the long lines; and the Rembrandt House.

The local architecture is both familiar and exotic. Along some canals, what a Charlestonian might call row houses dominate, tall and narrow and handsomely appointed. Though the streets are not without their share of old mansions, most are occupied by consulates, banks and other businesses.

If one wonders why so many businesses and houses have a block-and-tackle set-up depending from top-floor gables, it's because the doors and staircases of Amsterdam are notoriously narrow. Families on the move ship their furnishings and other belongings into and out the windows.

The custom or makeshift houseboats one sees moored along many sections of the canals are not mere decoration. The city suffers from an acute housing shortage, and space is at a premium. Yet to the wanderer on foot or on bike, nothing seems crowded — until you reach the fabled Red Light District.

The Glow

OK, OK, the Red Light District. We were getting to it. If you are expecting seedy and dangerous, you're in the wrong place. Clearly marked by metal pillars with a rosette of LEDs, it inhabits the most beautiful part of the city, especially at night.

Apart from the legion of bars and restaurants, the streets are filled with everything from loud, boisterous young men showing off for each other to couples, families and new moms pushing strollers.

The reddish-orange neon portals and the ladies beckoning from within seem like just another tourist attraction, as do the (wink, wink) "coffee" houses, but the reality is not quite what the imagination might conjure. These coffee shops emerged on a large scale when the city decriminalized marijuana in 1976, and it remains their chief (well, only) product, but it's still not expressly legal. It's just ignored.

That said, last April the government announced it intends to pass legislation to restrict the sale of marijuana to local patrons, allegedly avoiding imported crime. Cities such as Maastricht have banned foreigners from coffee shops since 2005.

Updating for 2016, especially potent cannabis (more than 15 percent of the active ingredient THC) soon may be reclassified as a "hard" drug and subject to stiff penalties, while the government also has compelled coffee shops where marijuana is sold to choose between alcohol and pot. Many have chosen the latter, with more than 100 of the previous 300 known shops having changed emphasis. Police crackdowns also have meant that organized crime has gotten involved. But the whole thing is as muddy an affair as ever.

When to go

If you fancy rubbing elbows with the tourist throngs and daytrippers from other parts of the Netherlands, time your visit for Queen's Day (April 30), the celebration of the queen's birthday. But make certain you've made hotel reservations well in advance. It's a mad house.

April is the best time of year to take in Keukenhof Gardens in nearby Lisse. It is renowned as the world's largest flower garden, a tapestry of tulips and dozens of other varieties so vivid it has to be seen to be believed. Half-day and full-day tours are offered from Amsterdam.

Language is no problem in the Netherlands. The Dutch put most of us to shame linguistically. Most speak three or four languages — fluently — and English is so pervasive that asking a local if he speaks it is a minor affront.

For all practical purposes, "Holland" and "the Netherlands" are interchangeable terms, but if you want to impress the townsfolk, make the distinction. Divided into north and south provinces, Holland actually is an area in the Netherlands. And Amsterdam is the centerpiece of the north.

All in all, a very broad-minded, fun-loving centerpiece.

CHAPTER 10

The Spirit of Place

The Spirit of Place

"We travel not to escape life, but for life not to escape us."
– Anonymous

The word "authenticity" is an increasingly nebulous, or at least debatable, term. What does it actually mean in this day of overwrought travel advertising? Much is made of alleged artistic, culinary or cultural authenticities that are, in fact, comparatively recent variants on tradition. This does not mean that they are without value or interest, just that it's more marketing than substance, the hype machine working overtime to promote what is many countries' bread and butter: tourism.

One thing "authentic" does not mean is "unchanging," despite the connotation of the word. Nothing exists in stasis, not the most storied dishes of classical French cuisine or the contours of the Grand Canyon. Something to keep in mind when regarding celebrations in the present of revered signposts of the past. Even the spirit of a place is not truly timeless, but it can seem so.

Oft aligned with "authenticity" is the notion of the bucket list, with no end of books, websites and magazine articles touting the 10, 100 or 1,000 things to do/ places to see before you die, most pushing the concept of genuineness. Having a wish list for travel is one thing — mine is added to or revised on a monthly basis — but a checklist something else. It is a trap that's all too easy to fall into, and you wind up treating a journey or journeys as part of a log of tourist "experiences" to complete, no matter how superficial they might be.

Is the Great Wall of China *authentic*? The Coliseum in Rome? They are genuine, certainly. Concrete and reliable edifices that draw millions of amazed gawkers. But what of coastal fishing villages of Ecuador? The Manhattan skyline? That Pad Thai you had for dinner last night? Just what is authentic, anyway?

You can argue that this is a game of semantics, easily manipulated. But a lot of the chatter about authenticity is doggerel fixating on an illusion.

In reviewing Philip Marsden's *Rising Ground: A Search for the Spirit of Place*, the great travel writer Jan Morris lamented that the art of literary travel writing is dying out, a victim of how-to books on the prosaic end of things and of "transcendentalisms" of one kind or another —"transformed by a generation of writers concerned less with travel itself than with its deeper implications — places as ideas rather than facts."

Much ink has been spilled trying to define what we call "a sense of place" or the "spirit of a place," with exponents of cultural and religious history emphasizing beliefs involving the sacred character of specific places (drawn from Latin *Genius loci,* or guardian deity of a locale). These are ritual landscapes, locales whose topographical features or human construct have taken on, over years or centuries, some metaphysical character, as if inhabited by a godlike being, spirit or nature elemental. Such places — Stonehenge or Easter Island, for example — are wellsprings of all manner of ritual. This, and as Morris puts it, "the feeling that generations of emotion have left some vaporous sensation behind, perceptible still."

Now this is all rather ethereal, but it is important to recognize that (respectful) travelers are in many ways contributors to the spirit of place. And each one of us may apprehend it differently. The more secular or pragmatic view characterizes "sense of place" as those special sites or settings to which we respond based on a complex set of cultural preconceptions, suggesting that we reshape such places to embody those preconceptions, that "the sense of place" is really a state of mind we create rather than some intrinsic set of qualities.

Perhaps, but that hardly matters, does it?

Often, what draws us to a place is simply its strangeness. "A good traveler returns exhilarated, restored, and confirmed by the jolt of strangeness," writes Willard Spiegelman in the essay collection *Senior Moments.* "The most commonplace things are imbued with an exotic charge by the sheer fact of these varying degrees of unfamiliarity."

I am a product of place, and sufficiently strange to boot.

While my personality and perceptions may have been influenced by having grown up in North Carolina, and in the U.S., the fact is that no place — not Alaskan fjords, Parisian boulevards or the Great Barrier Reef — remains in a fixed, eternal state. Places, like people, change and evolve, and our response to place — apart from the most familiar touchstones — is equally as fluid. Analyze it all you like, but the point is to appreciate and enjoy it.

———————

Travel stories
Haunted Lands (2005)

St. George, Utah – The story of the Earth is told in rock.

And the tale of the American West is a primordial narrative, testament to the power of wind and water – to sculpt, to mold, to carve canyons.

Zion National Park is one of its masterworks, both geological museum piece and gallery.

State Road 9, coursing through the southern reaches of this haunted land, is hardly the road not taken. But it is certainly taken less often. While roads skirting the nearby Grand Canyon bustle with a current of cars, on SR 9, otherwise known as the Zion-Mount Carmel Highway, it is a trickle. Sometimes you are alone, as if transported into one those ludicrous car commercials, slaloming solo along a mountain blacktop, dust in your wake.

Here it's reality.

What the landscape may lack in immensity, it compensates for in drama. Although the narrow Kolob Canyons to the north also harbor miles of wilderness, approached off Interstate 15 (Exit 40), the central feature of the 147,000-acre park is Zion Canyon, hewn by the Virgin River over a period of 13 million years. The 25-mile section of highway winds east from St. George through sheer cream-and-red Navajo sandstone cliffs — monoliths as high as 3,000 feet — shaped and striated by millennia of erosion into elegantly rounded contours.

The Zion-Mount Carmel Highway is a breathtaking feat of human engineering cut through nature's artistry (and sense of mystery), with switchbacks climbing steeply from the canyon floor past petrified sand dunes, such as the famous Checkerboard Mesa. At sunset, well before the moon rises, chalky cliff faces seem reluctant to relinquish the sun's failing light, still bearing a ghostly luminosity.

By car, on foot

At the crossroads of Virgin, one may take an 18-mile detour along the Kolob Terrace Road to Kolob Plateau, where mesas and bluffs such as Tabernacle Dome and the two Guardian Angels command the eye. If time is short, remain on SR 9. By day, even brief hikes off this main road reward visitors with enchanted nooks and stirring vistas. The Emerald Pools and Weeping Rock trails offer two of the more frequented routes. For more solitude, and a most impressive view, there is the four-mile (round trip) Canyon Overlook Trail, located just past the second

Zion-Mount Carmel Tunnel.

Until fairly recently you could depart SR 9 at Rockville and motor north alone the seven-mile stretch of Zion Canyon Scenic Drive into the canyon itself. But this has been closed to car traffic. Now, you must take one of the guided tour trams to sites such as the Great White Throne. Continuous tram service allows you to dismount the bus and set out on one of the fine trails. Chief among them is the Riverwalk Trail, which leads to the Narrows, a gorge of sandstone arches, grottoes and fluted walls that lives up to its name. For this hike, be prepared and use caution. After a short distance, the maintained trail ends, and the route becomes the river itself. Currents can be treacherous, and once you've entered the canyon from its upper end, it is not so easy to backtrack.

Alternately, drivers piloting tough SUVs or other off-read vehicles can head south at Rockville toward Big Plain Junction on the Smithsonian Butte Backway, a bumpy nine-mile road crossing orchards and cattle pastures.

Backpackers who prefer hiking off the beaten track can venture north to the Kolob Arch Trail, which parallels Timber Creek — and drops almost 1,000 feet to La Verkin Creek — en route to a rock span measuring 310 feet, one of the largest free-standing arches in the world. The trail affords views of Hop Valley, Willis Creek and Beartrap Canyon.

Near the eastern limit of SR 9, a side trip to Coral Pink Sand Dunes State Park along Route 43 is well worth the time, moving through Kaibab National Forest with its huge Ponderosa pines and quivering aspens.

Botanical bonanza

Zion contains Utah's greatest botanical diversity, with almost 800 species, some cascading as hanging gardens from cracks and crags in canyon walls. Here, one finds golden and cliff columbine, maidenhair ferns and scarlet monkeyflowers. Higher, they give way to stands of aspen, juniper, live oak, white fir, pinyon pine and the majestic Douglas fir. In the lower realm, look for cholla and prickly pear cacti, desert sage and mesquite trees.

Animal life is no less abundant, but it takes patience to spot species such as the ringtail cat, roadrunner, beaver and mule deer. By contrast, bird life is everywhere. Bring your binoculars and gaze upon peregrine falcons, golden eagles and ravens. Other than the brawny but harmless chuckwalla lizard, reptiles are best avoided; the Great Basin rattler calls Zion home, too.

As with all natural areas, Zion's face changes with the seasons, from the spring's swollen rivers and waterfalls to the lush greenery and wildflower arrays of early summer, autumn's orange-gold palette and winter's snow-capped silences.

Temperatures vary with changes in elevation as well as seasons. Spring can be rather wet, summer hot (95-100 degrees) during the day but agreeably warm (65-70) at night. Afternoon thunderstorms, common from mid-July through mid-September, can generate flash floods. Fall days are usually clear and mild; nights are cool. Colorful foliage displays begin in September in the high country, but not until November down in Zion Canyon.

History

Zion was named for the heavenly city of God by 19th-century Mormon settlers, some 309 families having been dispatched south from Salt Lake City by Brigham Young in 1861 to plant cotton. It was one of Young's more enthusiastic pioneers, Isaac Behunin, who christened it after the hill in Jerusalem where the temple was built.

The park was established in 1919 to protect this geological marvel from further encroachment, and it remains the state's most popular despite competition from Utah's other uncommon wonders: Canyonland, Arches and Bryce Canyon national parks.

A visit to Zion easily can be expanded into a grand scenic loop. SR 9 ends at Mount Carmel Junction, where you can travel south on Highway 89 to Page, Ariz., just below the border. Page, located along the banks of picturesque Lake Powell, is a staging area for sojourns to mesmerizing Antelope Canyon, a "slot" canyon on Navajo land famous for sculptured inner walls that have the luster of amber or spun honey. Also nearby is stunning Horseshoe Bend, one of America's most photographed overlooks.

From Horseshoe Bend it's a comparatively short (by Western standards) drive on Highway 89 east past Vermillion Cliffs National Monument (with its own otherworldly terrain) and Marble Canyon, then up, up, up to the glorious North Rim of Grand Canyon National Park, 1,000 feet higher than the far more touristy South Rim, but inaccessible in winter. From the North Rim, simply take the sparsely traveled Highway 89 north back to Zion.

Resources

The Zion National Park Visitor Center at the southern entrance is located on SR 9 at Springdale. For information, call (435) 772-3256 for 24-hour updates, or e-mail the center via its website at www.nps.gov/zion. The Kolob Canyons Visitor Center in the northwest can be reached at (435) 586-9548. You can also go online at GORP (www.gorp.com), an all-purpose site with in-depth profiles (including hiking and camping guides) for all U.S. national parks.

During summer months, the visitor centers are open daily from 8 a.m.-7 p.m. Spring, fall and winter hours are shortened.

There is convenient lodging inside the park at the rustic Zion Lodge at Springdale—call (435) 772-7700—and a number of chain motels also are available near the park's western (St. George) and eastern (Kanab) approaches. To make a campground reservation, call (435) 772-3256.

It's not easy to enjoy our national parks and still avoid the crowds. Here you can. Drink it in. Perhaps you'll echo Isaac Behunin and exclaim "This is my Zion!"

Coastal Walks in Cornwall and Wales (2016)

CORNWALL, ENGLAND — Rugged is too tame a word to describe the windswept Cornish coast, a rocky peninsula jutting seaward at the southwestern extreme of Great Britain. The same wide beaches, high cliffs and spectacular vistas continue on its cousin to the north, the Pembrokeshire coast of Wales, which undulates like desert sands carpeted in green.

Together, they harbor as much visual drama as a hiker, cyclist or walker could want.

Both offer unspoiled scenery, abundant wildlife, quaint villages and bastions of historic and prehistoric grandeur. The inquisitive also will discover pockets of age-old cultures that cling to these outposts with obstinate, sometimes aloof, determination.

Celebrated in Lonely Planet as one of the great walks of the world, the Cornish Coastal Path can be taken in segments, with more than 90 detailed, generally circular walks that explore the complete shoreline of Cornwall. The walks embrace gentle stretches as well as blustery headlands, steep coastal valleys, sheltered estuaries, sequestered coves, moors and soft sand beaches.

Although the path actually begins well to the east at Cremyll, near the

English city of Plymouth, most walkers prefer to start in West Cornwall and head north. With so many options from which to choose along this 296-mile portion of the 630-mile South West Coast Path, guidebooks like those published by the South West Coast Path Association help with planning. Be warned: Cornwall is besieged by vacationers in summer.

If solitude is your aim, avoid the tacky destination of Land's End and begin your introductory walk just to the north at Old Lizard Head, where the "crowds" are all avian. Here, in a single week, may be spotted bird species such as cormorant, gannet, sparrowhawk, raven, magpie, razorbill, storm petrel, oystercatcher, whimbrel, herring gull, shearwater and a half-dozen others, not to mention the Atlantic grey seal.

Another fine walk is a challenging four-miler moving from the town of Looe through old oak woodlands and toppling down to Talland Bay, once a favored refuge for smugglers. Don't let the short distance fool you. It travels the shore like a roller coaster. Less ambitious souls will enjoy the Tintagel path, a five-mile circular walk which takes in Tintagel Church on the cliffs outside the village then travels various lanes parallel toward a descent to the cove of Trebarwith Strand.

Locals insist that Tintagel Castle, a medieval fortress, was the birthplace of the legendary King Arthur (or his historical surrogate).

For those unfamiliar with Cornwall, the chief surprise is its profusion of semi-tropical vegetation, which populates a host of lush gardens. Thank the Gulf Stream for the region's unusually mild climate and arable fields, which have captivated visitors and rewarded farmers for centuries.

There are any number of towns you can adopt as a base for your Cornish exploration, which also should include its Celtic heritage. Falmouth, with its museums, galleries, gardens and beach, may be chief among them. It also is the gateway to St. Mawes, a much-loved fishing village on the Roseland peninsula.

But equally well situated are hilly, picturesque St. Ives (famous as an artist's colony) and the somewhat more touristy shipping port of Penzance.

Traveling Cornwall will only whet your appetite for more. Namely, Wales.

Welsh "rare bits"

Established in 1970, and traversing 186 miles of breathtaking scenery, the Pembrokeshire Coastal Path (PCP) in rural Wales is a stunning maritime landscape rivaling our Pacific Northwest, from its precipitous limestone cliffs and volcanic headlands to sandstone coves, glacial valleys, broad beaches and rich estuaries.

Lying within Great Britain's lone coastal national park, the Pembrokeshire Coast National Park, the Path's many walks can constitute an easy stroll for families or a major test for the veteran hiker, its estimated 35,000 feet of ups and downs rather fancifully compared to scaling Mount Everest. But it, too, can be savored in sections that can be managed by anyone. Some 130 shorter circular walks are listed on the PCP's website.

The PCP is part of the larger Wales Coastal Path, an 870-mile-long walking route covering the entire Welsh coast from Chepstow to Queensferry. It attains its highest point at 574 feet. Most of the coastline faces west toward the sparkling Irish Sea, yet at different declinations surveys the landscape at every point of the compass. Spring and early summer usher in a bevy of coastal wildflowers, and the bird life is as profuse as Cornwall's. Sharp-eyed walkers also may spy seals and dolphins cavorting offshore throughout much of the year.

Likewise worth seeing are the sand and rock formations at Marloes, and the offshore wildlife reserves of Ramsey and Skomer Islands.

Pembrokeshire's cliffs are, if anything, even more dramatic than Cornwall's, and the winds can be fierce. Not least at Stackpole, a former estate that today is a National Nature Reserve. It is accessed most readily via the town of Pembroke and village of Lamphey, the latter home to a haunting ruin known as the Lamphey Bishop's Palace.

Also nearby the PCP are attractive seaside enclaves like Tenby and tiny St. David's on St. Brides Bay. While there are small hotels, B&Bs, cottages and guest houses along the way, backpackers tackling lengthier segments of the trail can opt for campsites, but are advised to carry their own food and water.

Getting around

Driving the pretty but notoriously narrow roads of the Cornish and Welsh coasts is not for the faint of heart. Many, bounded by "hedgerows" that are three inches of vegetation masking unforgiving stone walls, were designed for horse and cart, not modern automobiles or trucks. That doesn't stop the locals from zipping along them at heart-stopping speed. Good road manners are vital.

Fortunately, the entire PCP can be reached by varied bus services tailored to the needs of walkers, among them the St. David's Peninsula Shuttle Service and the cheekily named Poppit Rocket.

It's a coastal jaunt you'll never forget.

––––––––––

Coasting on Cumberland (1997, updated for 2016)

CUMBERLAND ISLAND, Ga. – Ambling through the sun-dappled interior, the first thing you notice is the silence, broken only by the wind sighing through live oaks, the call of a bird or the rustle of some small creature in the bush – a raccoon perhaps, or an armadillo.

Just at the edge of awareness is the sound of the surf, whooshing onto a broad, lonely beach that shoulders up to a bulwark of dunes.

As stealthy as a ninja, a white-tailed deer breaks from cover, crossing the wide footpath and disappearing into shadow. Splashes of color – cardinals, tanagers and pileated woodpeckers – show vividly against a canvas of green. High above the graceful contortions of the trees, with their cascades of Spanish moss, an osprey wheels.

You're alone. In the restorative embrace of Cumberland Island.

Breathe deeply.

This complex and varied ecosystem of maritime forest, saltwater marsh and beach encompasses the Cumberland Island National Seashore, accessible only by boat from the small coastal town of St. Mary's.

Georgia's largest and southernmost barrier island is, like Bull's Island on South Carolina's Cape Romain, an explosion of nature amid an oasis of quietude: 9,800 acres of wilderness veined with hiking trails and blessed with 18 miles of utterly undeveloped beach.

Apart from the modest Sea Camp visitor center, where backcountry campers can obtain carts to transport their gear, little evidence exists of human impact, save for the well-maintained network of narrow roads and trails. No cars, trucks, or sport-utes, thank you.

If not exactly unique among National Park System sites, the prohibition of motor vehicles on Cumberland Island is welcome. Only families who still own land on the island or maintain private residences there are excluded from the ban. Bikes are available for rent at the Sea Camp visitor center (first come, first served) and for guests of the Greyfield Inn on Cumberland Sound.

A rich history

Originally inhabited by the Timucuan peoples, a coastal tribe today found mainly in Florida, by 1610 the island was the locus of Spain's second-largest mission on the East Coast. Sea Island cotton was an important crop during the plantation period, which gave way to a clutch of mansions built by the Carnegie family in the 1880s.

Only ruins remain of the once-proud Dungeness, a four-story tabby home constructed by Catherine Greene, the widow of Nathanael Greene, in the 1890s and rebuilt on the old foundation by Thomas Carnegie and his wife Lucy. The ruins are best viewed from a distance, given the instability of the structures and the presence of three species of poisonous snakes.

In 1893 a settlement was established for black workers, and the First African Baptist Church was erected there. Rebuilt in the 1930s, it is one of the few surviving artifacts of this community.

No signs remain of Fort Andrews or Fort William, which once safeguarded British colonial interests. But Plum Orchard Mansion, an imposing Georgian Revival edifice built for George Carnegie and his bride Margaret in 1898, stands in all its splendor. Hard by the Brock Hill River, the home was donated to the National Park Foundation in 1971. Together with endowments from private sources it paved the way — or rather, planted the seed — for Cumberland Island National Seashore.

Come prepared

Cumberland Island boasts a typical subtropical climate of mild winters and summertime temperatures ranging from the low 80s to the high 90s. Rain gear is advised. Bring all the food and beverages you need, as well as the requisite insect repellent. Nothing is sold on the island.

The park service operates a passenger ferry twice daily, seven days a week. Outbound times from St. Mary's are at 9 a.m. and 11:45 a.m. Return trips are scheduled at 10:15 a.m. and 4:45 p.m. plus an additional 2:15 p.m. return trip available Monday through Saturday from March through Aug 31. The winter ferry schedule runs five days a week, with no service on Tuesdays and Wednesdays from Dec. 1 to Feb. 28. Advance reservations are required. Call (912) 882-4336.

When making ferry reservations, people with disabilities should request a "beach chair" – a wheelchair with oversized tires for easier movement in sand.

Squadrons of opportunistic cormorants and ring-billed gulls accompany your ferry across Cumberland Sound, breaking off only as you pass the island's south end marshes – festooned with white ibises – and reach either of the two simple docks: Dungeness and Sea Camp. Maybe you'll be lucky enough to spy a grazing manatee in this, the state's only "sea cow" preserve.

A good way to get the lay of the land is to study a map beforehand and take one of the 30-mile guided van tours led by park service naturalists. Then strike out on your own. There's a great deal of ground to cover, however, and day hikers should plan to take the early trip out. Otherwise, the few hours allotted will not afford a visitor much sense of the variety of terrain or ecosystem.

With enough time, walkers maintaining a brisk pace can cover most of the island's attractions in the course of one long day.

Camper's haven

But the best way to experience Cumberland Island is as a camper. You can choose between one developed and four primitive backcountry sites. Enthusiasts of roughing it definitely will prefer the latter.

Sea Camp Beach has restrooms, showers (cold) and drinking water. Campfires are allowed at Sea Camp, although only dead and downed wood are acceptable as fuel. Stafford Beach campground is smaller but also has restrooms and fire rings. Backcountry sites go by the names of Brickhill Bluff, Yankee Paradise and Hickory Hill and are sequestered in appealing spots. Inland, freshwater marshes and ponds provide drinking water for the native animals, but humans should treat any water taken there thoroughly. They also serve as alligator habitat, so have a care.

There's a seven-day limit on camping and reservations can be made up to six months in advance. Permits also are required. Three to four days may be optimum for most visitors, providing ample time to explore the island's flora and fauna.

It's alive!

Wildflowers carpet the paths from Dungeness dock to the beach, among them chokecherry and yaupon holly, violets and oxalis, which give way to prickly pear cactus in the open sand and scrub oak and myrtle in the dunes. The dunes rise as high as 40 feet on the west side of the island, looking down on majestic sweeps of beach where shorebirds such as the ruddy turnstone frolic.

Loggerhead turtles lay their eggs in the sand on Cumberland Island between April and August while the saltwater marshes are inhabited by sea trout, bluefish and lemon shark. Also to be found, or heard, in the marshes are cattle egrets, coots and clapper rails.

Camellias vie with the palmettos and oaks for dominion in the island's wooded center, where squirrels, opossums, owls and skunks join the aforementioned racoons and armadillos. To this day, no one really knows how the armored critters made it here.

It is unfortunate that people chose to introduce pigs and horses into this synthesis of interdependent environmental systems, for they have spawned feral populations that compete with indigenous wildlife for food – which is not to say that sighting a herd of wild horses lacks an aesthetic quality or surge of excitement.

Don't miss the wild north end. Stands of longleaf slash pines stake a claim here, their branches bedecked with chortling wrens, yellowthroats and buntings. On Cumberland Island, birdwatchers will believe they've reached nirvana.

The interior of the island offers shade from an unrelenting sun, but things can get a bit stuffy for hikers moving at a good clip. Those needing the resuscitation of a blast of sea breeze will find nine well-marked outlets leading from the trails to the beach.

Not enamored of sleeping bags? Try the Greyfield Inn, a storied B&B (www.greyfieldinn.com). Greyfield has its own private ferry that departs from Fernandina Beach, Fla. For reservations and other information, call (904) 261-6408.

CHAPTER 11
Touring the Southeast

Touring the Southeast

"The everyday kindness of the back roads more than makes
up for the acts of greed in the headlines."
– Charles Kuralt

The southeastern U.S. always has been my home, though I confess it has been as much by chance as by design. This is where I was born and raised. This is where the work was. And while I frequently envy those who have had the good fortune (or ambition) to live in some of the great large cities of the world, I have had the privilege, for the last 40 years, of dwelling in one of its finest small ones, Charleston, S.C.

Aside from savoring the area's indigenous pleasures, as Charleston has enhanced its allure as a tourist, historical, and culinary mecca, it has also enjoyed an expansion in airline routes, becoming an increasingly good staging ground for exploring other places in the South — a region that defies easy description, as well as old stereotypes.

Big, complex and sometimes elusive, the South still grapples with ancient problems, and there is much moonlight-and-magnolias nonsense served up by overripe novels, gushing travel magazines and the exaggerated claims of tourist bureaus. Some of the much-touted cosmopolitanism and gentility of its cities can be skin deep.

Yet many of the romantic images it conjures are quite real, extraordinarily evocative and enduring: misty mountains, vast hardwood forests, barrier islands, warm-water beaches, opulent gardens, majestic live oaks, stunning sunsets, and seductive scents carried on an evening breeze.

Diverse natural beauty combines with thoroughly modern cities (as distinctly themselves as San Francisco or Chicago), burgeoning arts and entertainment industries, an inexhaustible array of historical sites, and destinations aplenty for adventurers and wildlife watchers of every stripe.

Scenic highways abound.

In recent years, a culinary revolution has come South, coexisting or interacting with traditional foodways to create a gastronomical wonderland of flavors and styles. I'm happy to say that Charleston is widely celebrated as the standard bearer of this awakening, but great chefs have flocked to the region, conjuring culinary magic that knows no borders.

Like all places, what is background to a native is exotic to a traveler, particular a first-time visitor, and the oft-celebrated hospitality of the region is, for the most part, alive and thriving. We appreciate you coming, not least because it helps us see our own home through fresh eyes.

Travel Stories
Mysterious Lake Waccamaw (2010)

LAKE WACCAMAW, N.C. -- Mystery still envelops Carolina bays, of which Lake Waccamaw is one of the largest and most picturesque.

An oasis of biodiversity with its own state park (and minimal intrusion by the lakeside town that shares its name), Lake Waccamaw offers a sparkling panorama on a sunny day and more than a few question marks.

Carolina bays, an estimated 500,000 in number, are inland elliptical depressions pocking the Atlantic coastal plain not only in the Carolinas but in Delaware, New Jersey, Virginia, Georgia and Florida. Maryland has the cheek to call theirs "Maryland Basins."

Named after the sweet bay, loblolly bay and red bay trees frequently found growing along their banks, Carolina bays, each aligned in a northwest-southeast direction and often appearing in groups, vary in size from 500 feet in length to several thousand acres.

Many are marshy, but a few – such as the 14-square-mile, 9,000-acre Lake Waccamaw, which has a maximum depth of 11 feet – qualify as lakes.

Some bays exhibit open water with large clumps of pond cypress, while others are composed of dense shrub (pocosins) with floating peat mats. Generally, but not always, the southeastern end has a higher rim revealing white sand "beaches."

Lake Waccamaw and Lake Waccamaw State Park harbor several species that are found nowhere else on the planet. Included are the fish species known as Waccamaw darter, Waccamaw silverside and Waccamaw killifish.

They are accompanied by a more familiar range of anglers' delights: largemouth bass, crappie, perch, bowfin and, near the mouth of the Waccamaw River, catfish.

While many bays are totally dependent on rainfall, Lake Waccamaw obtains its water supply from the Friar Swamp drainage.

Most Carolina bays also have naturally high levels of acid, drastically reducing the water's ability to nurture aquatic life. But limestone bluffs along Lake Waccamaw's north shore neutralize the acid, making the tea-colored water far more hospitable.

The lake also contains a range of unusual mollusks, with the Waccamaw spike and Waccamaw fatmucket among 15 species of mussels and clams found here. And of the 11 snail species, the Waccamaw amnicola and the Waccamaw siltsnail are exclusive to the lake.

Warm days bring inquisitive Carolina anoles and fence lizards to the shoreline, while the harmonies of spring peeper, Southern leopard frog, bullfrog and cricket frog dominate the night. Alligators also are in evidence, as are the more furtive white-tailed deer and fox. Bobcat and black bear are occasional residents, as well.

Bird life abounds. Brown-headed nuthatches, parula warblers and white-eyed vireos decorate the trees in the summer. In fall and winter, varied species of waterfowl prowl the lake.

Impressive. The question is, how did it get here?

Misty origins

Many theories have been advanced by scientists to explain the origins of these geological puzzles, no one of which is wholly accepted.

They fall into two principal categories: that they were created by forces within or upon the Earth, such as underground springs or wind and wave action, or that they were gouged by an astronomical event or set of events, such as meteor impacts.

It all gets rather technical.

Suffice it to say that no one really knows. Even radiocarbon dating and other techniques have proven to be unsuccessful at pinpointing the bays' age with certitude. Estimates range from tens of thousands of years to more than 100,000.

A bonus to visitors, just as fascinating if less mysterious, is the nearby botanical wonder known as the Green Swamp.

Designated by the U.S. Department of the Interior as a national natural landmark in 1974, the 15,722-acre Green Swamp Preserve encompasses pine savannas, bay forests and pocosins with hundreds of different plant species and animals such as alligator, Bachman's sparrow, the endangered red-cockaded woodpecker and Eastern diamondback rattler.

For more information on the Green Swamp, contact The Nature Conservancy.

Hiking

No one will confuse Lake Waccamaw State Park's lake trails with a Smoky Mountain ramble, but the terrain does offer much to see.

The longest in the park is the Lakeshore Trail, a five-mile (round-trip) walk that begins at the visitor center and follows the lakeshore to the Waccamaw River.

The trail passes through a variety of ecosystems, winding through a pine forest, under lofty hickory trees, past one of the oldest stands of cypress trees in the region, alongside grass beds in the lake that supply cover for fish and beside sandy beaches ideal for picnicking or simply taking it all in.

The Sand Ridge Nature Trail is a quick three-quarter-mile loop that begins and ends near the park's picnic area. Strollers can view reindeer and Spanish moss, reindeer lichen, pond pine, longleaf pine, turkey oak, laurel oak and hickory.

A 2.5-mile round trip, the Pine Woods Trail begins at the picnic area and offers its own botanical display, not least the famous Venus flytraps. Do not disturb, please.

Similar but shorter is the one-mile loop of the Loblolly Trail, which starts at the visitor center.

A particularly pleasant feature of Lake Waccamaw State Park is its boardwalk and pier. From a path leading out of the picnic area parking lot, the boardwalk winds 700 feet through bay forest, culminating in a 375-foot landing strip of a pier tailor-made for fishing and swimming. A smaller boardwalk traversing the forest is near the visitor center, sporting a pair of sun shelters.

There is no boat rental in the park or in town, but several public landings are available for folks who bring their own.

The town itself, with its handsome, unpretentious homes, pocket parks and array of private docks, is an inviting stroll. And some of the best lakeside views are to be had at the principal restaurant, Dale's Seafood – curious name for a place on a lake.

There's also the Lake Waccamaw Depot Museum (www.lakewaccamawdepot museum. com, admission free), a store of railroad artifacts that is on the National Register of Historic Places.

If you go

GETTING THERE: Lake Waccamaw State Park is in Columbus County, N.C.,

38 miles west of Wilmington and 12 miles east of Whiteville. From Interstate 95, travel southeast on U.S. 74, continuing east after it merges with U.S. 76. After passing Whiteville, travel approximately 12 miles. Signs on this highway will direct you to the park. **CONTACT:** Lake Waccamaw State Park, 1866 State Park Drive, Lake Waccamaw, NC 28450. Office phone: 910-646-4748, e-mail: lake.waccamaw@ncmail.netz. **PARK HOURS:** Open 8 a.m.-6 p.m. November-February; 8 a.m.-8 p.m. March-May, September and October; 8 a.m.-9 p.m. June-August. Park office hours 8 a.m.-5 p.m. daily (closed state holidays).

Little Grand Canyon

LUMPKIN, Ga. — It took the mighty Colorado River millions of years to sculpt the Grand Canyon, carving a mile deep through layers of limestone, shale, sandstone and gneiss. Georgia's Providence Canyon, by contrast, was formed in less than 200 years, due largely to poor farming practices in the early 1800s.

Rarely has human folly created something so strikingly beautiful.

Today, this unusual 1,103-acre state conservation park, oft dubbed the Little Grand Canyon, is a haven for hikers, backpackers, campers, picnickers and even passing motorists with only minutes to spare. Composed of soft, clay-dominated soils, and reaching a maximum depth of 150 feet, it is no less fascinating for being a series of 16 glorified gullies rather than a true canyon. Giving it dimension are knife-edged "promontories" jutting inward to abut mock "mesas" and "buttes."

If not for its dense stand of trees on the upper fringe and steamy canyon floor, Providence Canyon, with its rich earth-toned color palette, might seem plucked from the American West — Utah, say — and transplanted east, an incongruity until one understands what caused its formation amid the undulating hills and forests of southwest Georgia.

But park rangers say the canyon is only one of several such formations in the area, some of which are deeper and more extensive, though not as easily located or harbored on state-owned land.

When to go

Spring and early summer bring a riot of wildflowers, which enhance the canyon's variegated hues of ochre, pink, chalk white, red, orange and violet: 43 shades in all. The uncommon plumleaf azalea grows only in this region, blooming in July and August, while also in evidence are big leaf magnolia, passion flower and the trumpet creeper vine.

Prime season is in the fall, with a peak during mid-November. Go either at the beginning of the day or in the late afternoon for a chance to see the resident animal population of red fox, turkeys, Eastern cottontail rabbits, (nocturnal) armadillos and white-tailed deer. Sound effects include the tireless "drilling" for insects by local woodpeckers.

Photographers might want to devote an entire day to the visit, given how the character of the canyon changes with the light. Stargazers also flock here several times each year for the park's Astronomy Nights, sponsored by Columbus State University and the Coca-Cola Space Science Center.

Trekkers can savor canyon views from the easy rim trail or take the three-mile-long Canyon Loop to explore the canyon floor's nine accessible spur gullies (Nos. 4, 5 and 8 offering the best, most unobstructed prospects). Just prepare to have your boots muddied by shallow Turner Creek, a receptacle for loosened soil washed down by rain, which travels via the creek to the Chattahoochee River and eventually into the Gulf of Mexico.

Backpackers who venture out before 4 p.m. can stay overnight along the seven-mile Backcountry Loop, which is flecked with six campsites ($6 per person). But like its upstate cousin, Cloudland Canyon State Park at Lookout Mountain, one of the most impressive views of all is a few paces from the main picnic area.

Created in 1971, Providence Canyon State Conservation Park is on State Road 39C, just west of the hamlet of Lumpkin and 45 minutes south of the city of Columbus. It is open daily 7 a.m.-9 p.m. There is no entrance fee, but parking costs $5 per automobile (more for groups arriving in vans and buses). The park's Interpretive Center (8 a.m.-5 p.m.) offers a 13-minute video and exhibitions on the origin of the canyon.

Approximately one mile from the main park entrance are a pair of Pioneer Campsites for groups ($30, but no water or electrical hook-ups). There is also a group shelter that can seat 100 people.

Lodging

Camping ($22 per site) and cottages also are available nearby at picturesque Florence Marina State Park, the only lodging in the immediate area, set on 45,000-acre Lake Walter F. George (aka Lake Eufaula) 10 miles west of the canyon. Eight "dog friendly" efficiencies ($75/night) and six cottages ($100/night) are offered, plus a $3 parking fee. For reservations, call 800-864-7275 or 229-838-6870.

An enjoyable park in itself, Florence Marina sports a natural deep-water locus with a fishing pier, boat slips and boat ramp. Birders will spy herons, egrets and the occasional bald eagle. The park's Kirbo Interpretive Center informs visitors about Native Americans, nature and local history, and maintains displays of snakes, turtles, fish and artifacts from the Paleo-Indian period through the early 20th century.

Columbus is an appealing stopover/gateway city, roughly six hours by car from Charleston. Apart from the pleasures of its scenic 15-mile-long River Walk, which follows the east bank of the Chattahoochee (great for runners and cyclists as well as strollers), Columbus offers much in the way of the arts, not least the impressive Columbus Museum.

This complex features works by Winslow Homer, Robert Motherwell, Robert Henri and Dale Chihuly as well as regional painters and sculptors, exhibits of decorative arts, Native American crafts and Chattahoochee Valley history.

Close by are the River Center for the Performing Arts, the Coca-Cola Space Science Center, the National Infantry Museum at Fort Benning, the National Civil War Naval Museum and the restored Springer Opera House. The latter is the State Theatre of Georgia, a 138-year-old Edwardian showpiece in which such notables as Oscar Wilde, Ma Rainey and Lillie Langtry once performed.

For more information on Providence Canyon, write to 8930 Canyon Road, Lumpkin, GA 31815. Or visit www.GeorgiaStateParks.org.

Unadorned Delights (2009)

BLACK MOUNTAIN, N.C. – An old Mack truck, its fire-engine red faded to a pale pallor, dominates an alleyway like a dragon in a cave. A venerable brute, it strikes a stalwart (if faintly belligerent) pose. Of all the quaint elements of town center, it's the only one that doesn't suggest a warm "welcome."

Maybe you just need to get on its good side.

A satellite of the more populous tourist destinations of Asheville and Hendersonville, N.C., tiny Black Mountain (population 7,511) offers unadorned pleasures in a simple, breezy setting, though not without signposts of sophistication.

Touted as the rhododendron capital of the Eastern U.S., it also is notable for its proximity to major attractions such as the Blue Ridge Parkway, Biltmore

Estate, Lake Lure and Chimney Rock State Park.

But why leave? A quiet weekend or fortnight in this Swannanoa Valley community is restorative all by itself.

Appealing mountain scenery, a variety of recreational activities (hiking, biking, golf) and an unhurried small-town feel are complemented by the customary assortment of gift shops, galleries and, most interestingly, Appalachian crafts stores brimming with the wares of local and regional artisans: hand-thrown pottery, fabrics, iron works and dulcimer making, among them.

Apart from the unassailable majesty of Western North Carolina barbecue, there are restaurants of wit and of substance, of culinary innovation in a casual atmosphere. Lodgings range from cozy cabins and cottages to handsomely appointed bed-and-breakfast inns, one of which, Arbor House (207 Rhododendron Ave., www.arborhouse.com), commands a picturesque spot overlooking tranquil Lake Tomahawk.

Though the lake is man-made and on the small side, families still will appreciate Lake Tomahawk's bucolic setting and jogging trail, together with an unobtrusive combination of its swimming pool, tennis courts, croquet and picnic areas. Not to mention its sizable flock of ducks. Just waking up to the lake every day, nestled in the embrace of mountains, is satisfying enough.

The area also hosts numerous seasonal festivals, among them the Sourwood Festival, Upbeat! (celebrating the mountain music heritage), LEAF Festival of music, Black Mountain Art and Craft Show, Old Leaf Pumpkin Fest and Art in Bloom. For an aggregate collection and for the performing arts, there are the Valley Museum and Black Mountain Center for the Arts, respectively.

Native sons and daughters who have made their marks include singer-songwriter Roberta Flack, former University of North Carolina-Chapel Hill and NBA basketball star Brad Daugherty and NFL quarterback Brad Johnson.

Called the "front porch" of Western North Carolina, the Swannanoa Valley originally was settled by the Cherokee Indians. Climate had to be one of the draws. Today, average temperatures register at a clement 62 degrees (fall), 54 degrees (spring), 72 degrees (summer) and 35 degrees (winter).

The visitor center is at East State Street and Richardson Avenue. Bike rentals are available at Epic Cycle, 828-669-5965.

For more information, go to www.blackmountainnews.com or www.exploreblackmountain.com.

CHAPTER 12
Places of the Heart

Places of the Heart

"Here in the corner attic of America, two hours' drive from a rain
forest, a desert, a foreign country, an empty island, a hidden fjord, a
raging river, a glacier, and a volcano is a place where the inhabitants
sense they can do no better, nor do they want to."
- Timothy Egan in *The Good Rain: Across Time & Terrain in the
Pacific Northwest*

There are places that burrow under your skin and take up permanent
residence. Nothing can dislodge them from your thoughts for very long.
They speak to you in ways other places do not.

For me, the Oregon coast and the Olympic Peninsula of Washington State are
such places.

I am a Southerner born and bred, and beyond that an Easterner, certainly
in background, experience and largely in sensibility, however one might
characterize that. But I do not yearn so much for the mountains and the sea
separated by piedmont, as in my home state of North Carolina, but rather
for the grand tableau of mountain and sea together. Of expansive vistas and
otherworldly scale.

This is the Pacific Northwest of North America. And forgive me if I tend
toward the romantic, for I am seduced and enthralled.

Something indefinable awoke inside me from the moment I first trod the
Oregon Dunes in 1992. It was late afternoon, with no one in sight. A gentle breeze
caressed the sands, the sun warm on my back. Suddenly there was a gust of wind,
like a storm front approaching, and I felt a rush of the primordial. But the sky
was clear. Only the cries of birds and the whoosh of surf far below pierced the
silence. It was, I must confess, an almost spiritual experience.

Since that first venture, I have traveled up and down the length of the Oregon
coast as well as inland. I have hiked long trails of the Olympic Peninsula's
rockbound headlands and wild, varied interior. I have explored Seattle, of
course, and Portland, admirable cities both. These led me to neighboring places
– the redwood forests of northern California, Vancouver and Vancouver Island in

Canada. Endless panoramas.

I come back whenever I can. Meanwhile, I often revisit my photographs, and the spell is always cast again. I pass through a portal into that place, and feel it anew.

Yes, it rains. It rains a lot. Mists can shroud the coasts like a dense blue foam. But few sights match the glistening Columbia River Gorge after a soft shower, or the lush, verdant world of the Hoh Rain Forest, one of so many beneficiaries of abundant moisture.

Casual travelers can simply come here in the dry season, should they wish. For my part, let it rain.

I have written earlier in this book of the spirit of place. That spirit breathes in the Pacific Northwest. Some think Yosemite or the Grand Canyon are the grand finales of nature's creation in North America. I think it is here. Just set me down overlooking Cape Perpetua, or near the base of Mount Rainier, or on the banks of Lake Quinault, and I am content.

We all have such places. Or should have. Our second homes, at least of the imagination.

Travel Stories
An Olympian Feat

PORT ANGELES, Wash. – Thrice blessed, Washington State's Olympic Peninsulas offers three dramatically different worlds: snow-topped mountain summits, rocky shores and misty rainforests – all within a stretch of 250 miles.

It's not just geophysical marvels like the Olympic Range that captivate. This land's history and place names also conjure the exotica of diverse tribal influences: Kalaloch, Elwha, Dosewallips, Queets, Sequim, Hoquiam.

Coastal rock carvings (petroglyphs) near Cape Alava give us relics of the whale-hunting Makah Indians who thrived on the peninsula for more than 2,000 years before mysteriously abandoning their land in the early 1900s. The first recorded instance of visitors from the European civilization was Sir Francis Drake's expedition in 1579.

There is some reason to believe that explorers from the Far East made it as far as the peninsula in 458 A.D., led by a Buddhist monk named Hwui Shan who represented the Liang Dynasty. This Chinese expedition is known to have landed in Mexico and traveled north, possibly as far as the Pacific Northwest.

It was not until the 18th century that whites in any numbers intruded on what historically had been a "native American" realm. Waves of Russians migrated across the Bering Strait, the Spanish ranged up from California, the British and eastern Yanks from Cape Horn. The sea otter's luxuriant coat occasioned the full-scale exploration, and exploitation, of the region.

Yet for all this activity, which commenced long before Lewis and Clark made their landmark journey, the interior of the Olympic Peninsula defied deep penetration — even by Indians — until the Seattle Press expedition of 1890 became the first to cross it.

A rumpled carpet

The heart of this improbable assembly of geology, flora and fauna is Olympic National Park, which owes much of its good fortune to President Theodore Roosevelt, for whom the Roosevelt elk was named.

Two days before leaving office in 1909, he signed a decree setting aside 600,000 acres of the Olympic National Forest as the Mount Olympus National Monument. And while hunting and logging continued, the decision set the stage for President Franklin D. Roosevelt to later protect one million acres, including the monument, as Olympic National Park. Hunting and timber cutting ceased abruptly.

Not so in the Olympic National Forest (ONF), which surrounds the park on three sides. Clear cutting continued well into the 2000s.

Though there is grandeur to be found in the ONF, and hikers in great numbers traverse trails above the tree line of the Olympic mountains, it is the park's untouched forests that remain a principal draw.

The Western hemlock, which can grow as high at 200 feet and attain a diameter of eight feet (a circumference of 27 feet), is but one of several leviathans in the park. Two other conifers, the world's largest Douglas fir, and the planet's most prodigious Sitka spruce, also reside here, as do the handsome Western red cedar and big-leaf maple. All owe their impressive dimensions to a generally mild climate (helped by the offshore Japanese Current), copious rainfall and, not insignificantly, their location relative to other trees and nutrients.

The vast rumpled carpet of trees is the largest remnant of a primeval wildwood that originally extended 3,000 miles along the Pacific coast and as far inland as the Cascade and Sierra mountain ranges. Standing near the crest of one of the Olympic Range's great peaks, of which 7,976-foot Mount Olympus is the monarch, one has the illusion it still does.

Port Angeles on the north coast is perhaps the best-situated spot to launch one's initial foray into the park's 600 miles of hiking trails. Hurricane Ridge Road, a picturesque 17-mile drive, gradually ascends to one of the park's best trailheads at Hurricane Ridge. Topographic maps are a must for serious backpackers.

Rain's reign

The Bogachiel is the wildest of the four temperate, as opposed to tropical, rainforests encompassed by the peninsula, which also embraces the Queets, Quinault and, most popularly, the Hoh.

By definition, a rainforest is one that absorbs at least 80 inches of rain a year, a level usually associated with the Amazon and other lushly vegetated tropics. Temperate rainforests are a great rarity – those inhabited by conifers rarer still – all of which makes Washington State's emerald peninsula so noteworthy. While this quartet of forests is drenched by up to 150 inches of rain a year, the rainy season is far from constant. Winter it wettest. But the late summer and early fall months can be bone dry with the added peninsula-wide advantage of fewer visitors – and no bugs.

Although the apparent riot of growth does not appear to be as ordered as it is, the dense but (generally) navigable rainforest trails reveal a complex structure with as many as three layers. The "ground floor" of the forest is, naturally, the densest of all – a skein of juvenile trees, vines, berry bushes, moss, herbs and ferns.

The aptly named white foamflower is, along with the pioneer violet and pink bedstraw, among the few plants that punctuate the prevailing green. Some naturalists insist they have discerned as many as 19 different shades of this lordly color, and an hour or two in the rainforests convinces you they're right.

Not all of the rainforest's understory is jungle-like. There are large, open, park-like areas where one may spy Roosevelt elk (the second largest land mammal of the Northwest coast next to the moose) and black bear (grizzlies never made it to the peninsula). Higher elevations in other parts of the park are home to one of the largest populations of mountain lion on Earth. Wildlife is protected from hunting today, but it is too late to save the already exterminated wolf.

Battered beaches

The drama, and potential perils, of the interior continues seamlessly to the sea. The Northwest coast is actually two coasts that meld at one spot, Cape Flattery, the far-northwest tip of our nation's most northwestern state, Alaska.

The often spectacular 600-mile-long Ocean Strip, almost entirely wilderness, is at the mercy of the Northwest's violent winter weather. The life of its tide pools is world famous, but watch your step.

Then there are the thousands of miles of variously curved and convoluted shore, which meander inland from the Pacific through the 15-mile-wide Strait of Juan de Fuca (where seals and killer whales are a frequent sight) into Puget Sound and Hood Canal.

Those fond of kayaking or canoeing may want to tackle a portion of the 150-mile-long Cascadia Marine Trail running from the Canadian border to Olympia at the base of the eastern peninsula. There are more than 100 campsites along its length. One of the more popular legs for day paddlers is the South Shore Segment from Boston harbor to Olympia.

Don't overlook the aquatic pleasures of Lake Crescent in the north, artistically carved by glaciers 10,000 years ago, or Lake Quinault in the south, which sports the comforts and exceptional cuisine of rustic Lake Quinault Lodge.

Getting there

You can reach the peninsula from Seattle (or from a port near Victoria, Canada) via a system of ferries that cross Puget Sound. Once on the peninsula, any number of access roads connect with 325-mile-long U.S. 101, the highway that loops the peninsula connecting its villages, towns and park entrances.

Alternately, you can head south on I-5 from Seattle, pass Tacoma and hit U.S. 101 just east of Olympia to get a more complete exposure to 101's delights. Apart from Port Angeles and Lakes Crescent and Quinault, the towns of Forks, La Push, Kalaloch and Sol Duc Hot Springs offer lodging.

That, and some of the world's most plentiful seafood.

The Oregon Coast: Beyond Compare

COOS BAY, Ore. – To stand on the Oregon Coast is to glimpse the threshold of time.

There are majestic vistas that will alter your concept of beauty, that stir the soul and make the heart sing. But the forces that have sculpted this dramatic landscape, which have shaped forests and carved great monoliths of rock from the basalt and sandstone cliffs, continue their inexorable work.

Buttressed by mountains of the Coast Ranges and pummeled by the Pacific Ocean's relentless surge of wind and wave, the 400-mile length of shore is bisected by U.S. 101 – the breathtaking Oregon Coast Highway – and punctuated by more than 50 state parks and national forests.

It is a paradise for touring by automobile, or, for the more intrepid, by bicycle.

From craggy promontories to scalloped tidal pools at the sea's edge, from ghostly rain forests and giant sand dunes to alpine-like meadows and meandering freshwater streams, the Oregon coast is truly beyond compare, matted and framed in one of nature's most spectacular artworks.

And in the distance, above the broad shoulders of the Coast Ranges, is the soaring blue skyscape of the Cascades, which contain some of the highest peaks in the continental U.S. On a clear day, all this can be seen from a single vantage point.

Only once, near Cape Arago in the south, does the undulating Coast Highway move slightly inland. But even here, winding backroads return you to the coast through lushly forested hills and estuarine grandeur.

It is not until you head north beyond Tillamook or reach the furthest extent of the south Oregon coast at Brookings that the familiar sprawl of gas stations, fast food and development holds sway. Civilization may intrude elsewhere, intermittently, but there is mile after mile of utterly desolate beach and fragrant timber. Untouched lands endure in reserves like Siskiyou National Forest and Kalmiopsis Wilderness, with countless hiking trails to usher you under their canopies.

At the very edge of the sea, all is pristine. Aside from the solitary lighthouse and the rare home set back upon some precipitous cliff, the lone structures to be found are the many visitors' centers and rest stop/overlooks, unobtrusively incorporated into the settings.

Cannon Beach and Tillamook offer lovely introductory venues of the Oregon (pronounced "Or-gan") coast, but the sights turn glorious when you pass through the town of Lincoln City and attain the high crests above Otter Rock and Otter Cliffs Loop.

While it lacks the abundance of high stacks that festoon much of the shore, the massive volcanic headland of Cape Perpetua on the central coast at Siuslaw National Forest offers perhaps the most impressive views, from beach level or on high.

Honeycombed with trails, Perpetua is a botanical wonderland guarded by towering Douglas fir, Sitka spruce and coastal oak. There are also hemlock, alder, red huckleberry, coastal pine and myrtlewood, with a wide, deserted beach below.

If there is one stretch of the coast that provokes genuine awe, it must be amid the 200-foot dunes of Oregon Dunes National Recreation Area, where massive rolling mounds of sand alternately (if incongruously) evoke the Outer Banks of North Carolina – and the Sahara. That is, if they had the Adirondacks at their back. No more than a quarter mile behind the upper dunes rests a pastoral camping area of quiet glades and softly gurgling brooks, impossibly green terrain that – by an Easterner's reckoning, at least – should not exist within hundreds of miles of the camel-backed slopes of dune, much less hundreds of feet.

Outside the major timber port (and seafood spectaculars) of Coos Bay, just south of the sleepy fishing village of Charleston on the Cape Arago State Highway, is Shore Acres State Park. A literal stone's throw from the picturesque sweep of its Sunset Bay and Crescent Beach is Shore Acres Botanical Gardens, a unique and unexpected amalgam of horticultural styles featuring a riot of rhododendrons and roses.

Follow this alternate route another few miles to its terminus at Cape Arago and savor, near Florence, the most cacophonous of symphonic concerts at Sea Lions Caves. It is both the largest sea cave and cavern in America and the only year-round rookery on the U.S. mainland where Steller sea lions still dwell. Offshore rocks harbor large colonies of the braying, sublimely unconcerned creatures on narrow strips of beach, joined by choruses of cormorants and gulls.

At binocular range, gray whales may be spotted through the mists on their long migrations between the Arctic and their mating grounds in Baja California.

Backtrack a bit and return to U.S. 101 via the traditional loggers' trail that is Seven Devils Road. And take a few moments to stop at the South Slough, southernmost arm of the Coos Bay Estuary: 4,000 acres of salt marshes, tidal flats, open water and upland forest.

The lower coast also serves as gateway to one of the region's finest white water rivers, the Rogue. Jet boats stationed at Gold Beach take passengers along the old mail routes upriver on scenic, and often tumultuous, round-trip day rides. Bear, elk, and seabirds abound. Allow at least eight hours for the trip.

If time permits, consider a second side trip well inland, the majority of it along the exceptionally scenic state Highway 138 to Crater Lake National Park, which holds one of the great natural wonders of the world, 2,000-foot deep Crater Lake.

Back on the coast, a corridor of sheep and cattle ranches leads to the last of Oregon's extraordinary environs at Harris Beach State Park. Just north of Brookings, the park encompasses the first leg of 24 miles of flat gray sand chiseled by waves. Here are some of the most astonishing stacks to be found anywhere along the coast, rows of quasi-Gibraltars jutting from deep azure waters into an evening sky of pink, purple and ochre. To walk among them at low tide is to feel like a Lilliputian among Gullivers.

For ease of entry and exit into coastal stops, drive north to south from Portland — which allows for a splendid side trip east on old Highway 30 through the stunning Columbia River Gorge — and avoid much of the enormous buildup beginning at Oregon's northernmost coastal town of Astoria.

Past Brookings, you may also decide to cross the border into California to behold the 40-mile-long Redwood Highway and Redwood National Park. Groves of 300-foot-tall coastal redwoods, first cousin to the Giant Sequoias, have been ascending the skies for thousands of years, nourished by the coastal fogs.

For that matter, travelers can begin their journey in the Seattle area and either head west to the expansive Olympic Peninsula or east to Mount Rainier, then south to Portland and beyond. These additions will add 400 to 500 miles to your trip, but they will be unforgettable ones.

Famous (or infamous) for its rain, weather in the northwest varies considerably. Among the driest and most spring-like times of the year is late summer, with temperatures averaging in the mid-60s, though 80-degree days are not uncommon. Even during this time of year, bring a jacket if you plan to explore the dunes region; winds can howl unmercifully.

This much is guaranteed, you will not depart this land unmoved.

CHAPTER 13

Airbnb, Home Swaps and Family Travel

Airbnb, Home Swaps
and Family Travel

"People don't take trips. Trips take people."
– John Steinbeck

My personal preference in urban travel is for a venerable center city hotel where everything is a stroll away. There tend to be fewer unwelcome surprises. But rural excursions and villages where no small inn is available may call for a different approach. As does a city trip for those who prefer a "homey" atmosphere.

By now, most people are aware of Airbnb, an online community marketplace connecting people looking to rent their homes with people who are searching for agreeable accommodations. It has become something of a phenomenon, opening avenues in 192 countries at last count. One can rent by the night, week or month in most cases.

And it's no longer just about budget lodging. Yachts, houseboats and even castles can be rented, if that's your thing. But the smart traveler will want to make sure he or she is near the center of the action, failing easy mass transit from point to point. Just create a profile on www.Airbnb.com to get started.

For most people it's a win-win deal: Travelers get to meet local residents, pay less than the cost of a standard hotel room, and enjoy a more personal lodging experience. But as a potential guest in someone's home, you should be aware that properties don't always match their descriptions, and that some hosts can be less than hospitable. Airbnb tries to minimize problems through use of profiles, reviews, Verified IDs, messaging, secure payment platform and the Host Guarantee.

Extended stays in another domestic city or foreign country may call for house swapping (as celebrated in the fanciful 2006 film "The Holiday") or home stays. For the former, www.LoveHome Swap.com offers the most extensive home exchange website, featuring 75,000 properties in more than 160 countries, while www.homeexchange.com has been in business since 1992 and lists some 65,000 properties. For the home stays, there are a bunch of websites to explore such as www.homestay.com, with a database of 50,000 homes available in 150 countries. With both house swapping and home stays, there are many online alternatives to tap.

All these options have things to commend them.

A Word on Family Travel

This book focuses chiefly on travel for individuals and couples, but I would be remiss not to at least mention that family travel represents a big travel industry push these days, and that attractive deals are out there for the whole brood. And most of the same principles of successful travel apply.

The late humorist Robert Benchley, doubtless speaking for those who abhorred traveling with their families, quipped that "In America, there are two classes of travel: first-class and with children."

Perhaps in his era, family travel *was* limited, and a royal pain for people who preferred to be footloose and unencumbered. But it needn't be that way now.

Great gambols and even global adventures do not exclude family participation. Far from it. In this day and age, family travel offers just about anything your imagination can invoke (and your pocketbook can manage). Parents looking for something out of the ordinary can find it at the tip of a mouse.

The definition of "family" has likewise evolved, from unconventional assemblies of disparate types to multi-generational caravans savoring something more than traditional summer vacations. Whether a weekend getaway or a far-flung adventure, the possibilities are greater than ever. There are properties that cater specifically to families.

Sources of ideas include the revamped website www.familytravel.com, www.parents.com and www.familiesgotravel.com, but there are numerous sites to investigate.

––––––––––––

Travel Stories
Windswept history (2016)

BUXTON, N.C. –– On windswept Cape Hatteras, with its prominent "elbow" jutting seaward toward Diamond Shoals and its fabled lighthouse still a towering sentinel, the sense of vulnerability, of being on a slender spit of land way out in the Graveyard of the Atlantic, is not the immediate sensation.

No, you have to nurse that notion to make it real – or be here when a major storm lowers the boom.

As one strolls the beaches, casts a line, or motors along the grand, lonely stretches between townships, North Carolina's Outer Banks seem like any other chain of barrier islands: mutable yet eternal.

For thousands of years this broken strand has withstood onslaughts of wind and ocean, surviving as a restorative ecosystem of beach, sand dune, marsh and woodland, much of it encompassed by the Cape Hatteras National Seashore.

It is also a bastion of history.

The Italian explorer Amerigo Vespucci was among the first Europeans to set foot on the Banks in the 16th century. Four hundred years later, the wreckage of ships destroyed by German U-boats washed up on the same beaches.

The most famous of all pirates, Blackbeard, once terrorized shipping from his base at Ocracoke. And the wreck of the Civil War-era ironclad Monitor rests off Hatteras Island.

The very emblem of the Outer Banks, the Cape Hatteras Lighthouse (1870), is the tallest brick beacon in the nation at 208 feet. It was nearly claimed by the Atlantic Ocean before being rescued in 1999, when the entire structure (with its trademark spiral motif) was transported a half-mile farther inland to safety.

Tourist attractions here have been well-chronicled: the four lighthouses; the monuments to flight at Kitty Hawk and Kill Devil Hills (named after the rancid tasting rum that washed ashore after shipwrecks); the playground that is Nags Head; the lush Elizabethan Gardens; restored Waterside Theatre (home of "The Lost Colony"); Freedman's Colony; and the N.C. Aquarium on Roanoke Island.

Also: the "quaint" village of Ocracoke, the Dare County Civil War Trail, the Chicamacomico Lifesaving Station Museum, the fine Graveyard of the Atlantic Museum, the Native American Museum and Natural History Center in Frisco, the art galleries, a lengthy list of annual festivals and more.

Each has its charms, but to experience the Outer Banks minus the adornments and disconcerting development sprawl, wander away from the towns and into the wild areas along the 70-mile-long, 30,000-acre National Seashore, the first so designated in the United States.

Stretching between Oregon Inlet to the north and the village of Rodanthe to the south is the pearl of Hatteras Island, Pea Island National Wildlife Refuge.

The 6,000-acre refuge harbors 360 species of birds with the spring-to-autumn period being the most conducive to sightings. Laid-back hikers will enjoy an easy portion of the vast Charles Kuralt Trail. Guided canoe tours also are available for a fee.

Jockey's Ridge State Park near Nags Head sports the Banks' giant sand dunes, the largest on the East Coast and long favored by hang-gliding enthusiasts. For the past 38 years, the park has hosted the annual Hang Gliding Spectacular, billed as the world's oldest continuous competition.

Steady and consistent winds, temperate weather, shallow sound waters and rolling sea waves make the Outer Banks a prime locale for windsurfing, parasailing, kitesurfing and kiteboarding, kayaking, power skiing, offshore or inshore charter fishing and sailing.

The more sedate, however, can get their kicks cycling (there are paved and unpaved bike paths), shelling and surfcasting. Many a world-record fish species have been landed on or off the Banks over the years, not least the massive black drum. The Banks also offer seven fishing piers for those who like the company of fellow anglers.

Between Oct. 1 and April 30, those piloting off-road vehicles have multiple access points along the National Seashore where they can seek out their own private corner for fishing or a bonfire. Permits are required in some cases. For details, visit nps.gov/caha or www.outerbanks.org.

Birdlife also rules at the Bodie Island Marshes hard by Bodie Island Lighthouse, within the maritime forest of 968-acre Buxton Woods (part of the N.C. Coastal Reserve, with seven hiking trails) and in the Nags Head Woods Preserve.

For many, one of the principal pleasures of the Outer Banks is in getting there, especially from the South. Ferries linking the mainland departure points of Cedar Island and Swan Quarter with Ocracoke Island leave numerous times daily, offering a 2 1/4-hour cruise across the waters of Pamlico Sound for a $15 fee (2016) for cars, more for larger vehicles. You'll feel like you're well out to sea, accompanied by a cordon of gulls.

The free 40-minute Ocracoke to Hatteras/Hatteras to Ocracoke ferries leave with even greater frequency. Reservations are strongly recommended for the Cedar Island or Swam Quarter routes. Call 800-293-3779 or visit www.ncferry.org for schedules and further details.

Lodging and camping options can be assayed through www.outerbanks. org (or call 877-629-4386), which also offers an Outer Banks Getaway Card good for a 15-percent discount on rates at many motels, B&Bs, rental cottages and campgrounds.

You may choose to stay in a busier spot, complete with restaurants and taverns, but there are few places left on the East Coast where you can find a beach – and a primordial feeling – all your own.

CHAPTER 14
Mirage and Reality:
Travel Wisdom

Mirage and Reality: Travel Wisdom

*"Avoiding danger is no safer in the long run than outright
exposure. The fearful are caught as often as the bold."*
– Helen Keller

On Seeing Clearly

The first thing a wise traveler jettisons is the notion that you can escape
yourself through travel.

You may elude prejudice and preconception, grandiose idylls and romantic
illusions, but never yourself. For as the sage said, "Wherever you go, there you
are." Or as Ralph Waldo Emerson put it, "Though we travel the world over to find
the beautiful, we must carry it with us or we find it not."

Horace agreed, saying, "Those who race across the seas are changing their
skies, not their souls," suggesting that in our itch to travel, we belong nowhere,
and thus everywhere, a somewhat different notion of being a "citizen of
the world."

Yet as I have tried to stress throughout this book, a by-product of travel can be
finding one's self, redefining one's identity, obtaining a larger view of the world.
And a little strangeness is stimulating.

After all, do you really want to feel "at home" when you're abroad?

The biggest lesson is this: Instead of thinking about how things should be,
accept them for what they are. You have little choice, really. There is often a
considerable discrepancy between what the travel guides say a place will be like
and what it actually *is* like. Do you want predictability?

Be mindful of what you are seeing. As I have noted elsewhere, there are
opposing schools of thought in this regard. One insists that it is only when you
have experienced a place multiple times that you come to know it, and that
visiting, say, one museum or church a dozen times is infinitely more rewarding
than visiting a dozen museums or churches just once. I may agree in principle,
but object in practice. Traveling to the same place again and again has its appeal,
and certain advantages. Yet where is the adventure in repeating old successes?

Ibn Battuta journeyed 29 years (1322-1356) through the Middle East, Asia and Africa, an estimated 75,000 miles all told, and was regarded as among the most successful travelers in history. As far as we know, from Mecca to Beijing, he went to each place only once. Casting a wide net can mean a greater breadth of experience — if you arrive armed with knowledge, focus and the capacity to see perceptively.

For example, Russell Banks has argued that the great national parks of the world engage in some visual sleight-of-hand, centering on grand, sweeping mountain top vistas, deep canyons and vast stretches of water in an effort to play with scale, thus deluding the viewer into feeling exalted. In his book *Voyager* he contrasts this with the Everglades, a more humbling experience best seen at ground level and at human scale, on a more "interactive" basis. I understand what he means, but disagree with the notion that in visiting, say, King's Canyon and Sequoia National Parks in California, Cape Point in South Africa or Patagonia's glaciers one is being captivated by illusion. To me it's just apples and oranges, with both having their intrinsic values.

One presumption that usually *is* illusory when it comes to travel is the adage that "you get what you pay for." It may hold true when you reserve a decent $100-a-night hotel room as opposed to a super-cheap fleabag. But in a broader sense, money has little to do with having a great travel experience.

I'm definitely a fan of the Back Door Travel Philosophy, which, girded by its "cocky optimism," holds that in many ways the less you spend the more you get, that profligate spending on luxuries is not an investment in experience, but a blockade separating you from experience. Like most homilies, this is not always the case. But it is true often enough that we should be reminded of it. It does not necessarily mean traveling on the cheap — though this has undeniable virtues — but it does mean living in the moment, traveling intelligently and with a sense of proportion, recognizing that you can have a more direct, unfiltered journey when you rely on your own resources more than the service industry.

When Travel goes awry

The glamor of travel is seen only in retrospect, just as memory tends to store pleasant experiences and forget the pain.

Occasional discomfort and inconvenience are the fees paid for the pleasures of travel. But now and then a minor snafu morphs into a major headache. Sometimes you can just ride it out. Sometimes it threatens your trip. You can succumb to anger and frustration and bewilderment or, assuming there is a way out, you can try to find a way to circumvent or even eliminate the problem.

This is one area where the digital age delivers on its promise. Your cell phone or tablet computer can be a useful tool. But your chief ally is attitude. Resiliency is about meeting the worst life has to deliver with the best in ourselves. And there are little psychological gambits that can be utilized to lessen the irritation. To paraphrase Louis Wu, protagonist of Larry Niven's great "travel" novel *Ringworld*, I have to get over this sooner or later, so I may as well start now.

I once lost my passport in Venice. This, after a day of visiting half the attractions in the city. Before calling the Embassy, I decided to retrace my steps. It was an annoyance, to be sure, and the feeling of being overwhelmed and vulnerable was not pleasant. It was also on the only guided group tour I had taken, or have since, and I worried that I'd be holding things up or miss out, since the tour had another three or four cities to go.

My companion counseled me to be calm and patient, and my naturally methodical inclinations took hold. After returning to five places we'd visited during the day, we located a waiter at a restaurant who said he'd found my passport on a table and had shipped it over to a local police station. After a slightly uncomfortable half hour there proving my identity to dubious young officers, I was back on my way, passport in hand, and relieved. Total time lost: two hours.

Admittedly, this was a comparatively trivial setback, but it could have become something worse. You get the point.

Encountering real trouble

Being in a city or country when simmering strife boils over into trouble can be as fascinating as it is frightening. Suddenly, you are experiencing a place the way a foreign correspondent sees it when that place is in the grip of political tumult or war. Somewhat perversely, if you keep your head and don't take stupid risks, you may harvest an unforgettable memory. You are an eyewitness to events.

Granted, this outlook has an unpleasant whiff of the mercenary. No one should wish such miseries and dangers on a people just for one's own entertainment. But if you are already on hand, and there is no way to make a safe and graceful exit, you may as well observe the scene from a relatively secure position. You need not be intrepid, just cautious.

On Travel Guidebooks and Magazines

As you will see in the next chapter, I am a devotee of the great travel books, most of which have little to do with how-to advice. At the same time, I do admire those travel writers, like Rick Steves, whose principal goal in his books and TV shows is to provide useful information in an entertaining way. The same holds for the top online bloggers.

And it is hard to go wrong with the latest editions of such stalwart travel guides as those published by Lonely Planet, Fodor's, DK, Frommer's and National Geographic Traveler.

Although there are conspicuous exceptions, I am less enamored of the general run of travel magazines, especially the glossier ones. Sometimes, one subscribes to a travel magazine for a year in the same way one engages in a measure of hard-core roughing it, inviting boredom and a bit of hardship to unearth a few nuggets of enlightenment.

But with too many of these glossy publications, the chief takeaway is how to squander obscene amounts of money and shield yourself from real experience.

I've nothing against celebrating hedonism and a bit of self-indulgence, but some magazines exalt it to a fault. Better they should call their rag *Luxe Travel*, or *How to Spend a Small Fortune in the Most Conspicuous and Profligate Way Possible While Absorbing Little of Enduring Value*.

All-inclusive resorts may be fine as an occasional fantasy getaway and lavish "safari" camps where all one's desires are catered to at least are sufficiently well-run that you get to observe some amazing wildlife close-up. But they are not exactly wellsprings of authenticity. Rarely do they offer even a scrap of cultural truth. Again, why on earth would you go to a far-flung locale and stay in a mega-chain hotel, for heaven's sake, or be cloistered at any of the over-opulent Americanized lodgings? In this notion of travel, the only real contact with the locals one is likely to have is with "the help" (let's face it; that's how they are regarded much too often).

To be fair, doubtless some resort-goers do use these bastions of exclusivity as "base camps" to explore the country they are visiting and at least attempt to engage (respectfully) the people who are their hosts. But I suspect most are rather timid about pushing boundaries and merely want to recline in the lap of luxury and pretend they've actually seen Mali or the Yucatan or Tanzania.

Too often, the travel articles one sees in these periodicals have all the depth and subtlety of a fashion magazine. This is not a compliment. It is mainly about glitzy surfaces, not substance. As for anything resembling actual news, they are almost always late to the party, their "scoops" already stale.

There's much too much trafficking in bald-faced promotion, in the trendy nonsense of "Best Of" issues with their shallow Top 10 "rankings," little more than public relations boilerplate about what's allegedly "hot," with breathless, gushy writing — prose more suited to a teen magazine.

I would acknowledge that there is room for all manner of travel magazines, aimed at every conceivable predilection and personal style. But when the product reflects a readership that is status obsessed and spiritually bankrupt, how valuable, or useful, can it be?

Coda

We always wish we were a little better at realizing our passions, a little more ambitious. As a traveler, I have at times berated myself for not being daring enough, or adventurous enough, for not living up to the ideals often expressed in this book. But it should be remembered that they *are* ideals. States to aspire to, occasionally to attain, not be ruled by.

The fact is that some of the most celebrated travelers in history were self-absorbed, emotionally inert, prejudiced, neurotic or chronically ill. Among the travel writers, some facts are fudged, some "exploits" purely the stuff of fantasy.

In many places of the world, and not just the rural or remote, a traveler is a suspicious character, potentially inimical, an outsider at best. Which makes that traveler vulnerable, if not easy prey. Which is all the more reason to alloy caution with openness, to be respectful and polite and trust in your fellow humans to treat you with decency. More often than not, they will, sometimes with astonishing generosity. Of course, it is easy to write this, not so easy to live it. But that, too, is part of the traveler's education.

There is no litmus test you must pass to become a traveler, for the very reason that there are many different kinds. Be *your* kind of traveler, whatever that is. Stretch your limits, gradually but insistently. Savor the opportunities you have. After all, we travel not to escape life, but for life not to escape us.

CHAPTER 15

Great Books
on Travel

———

Great Books on Travel

You should abandon yourself to a travel book in the same way you abandon yourself to travel.

As with all reading, however, it pays to be selective. Unlike a travel article in a newspaper or magazine, which can be filled with specific advice on lodgings, restaurants, sightseeing and so on, the classic travel book is about one person's experiences over the course of a brief or years-long journey, seldom intended as a guide for others to follow.

It is about the writer, usually traveling alone, and the place (or places). It chronicles successes, failures, trials and triumphs — but not annual weather patterns or the best roads to take.

This does not mean there is nothing to learn from such books that will assist in your own travels.

Quite the contrary. Be it customs, language, history or foodways, you will learn a great deal more than in how-to or where-to guides, and not simply about travel.

Paul Theroux, an avatar of solo travel if ever there was one, counsels us that in the greatest of travel chronicles the word "alone" is an almost palpable presence. As far as he is concerned, arriving alone in a strange place, preferably rural and at night, is not a bewildering experience, but the essence of travel. If you only the vaguest plans for the days to come, so much the better.

Waking up in a strange place, not knowing what the day will bring, is real freedom.

Be warned: Some of the most vivid travel books involve ordeals, such as Jon Krakauer's masterful 1999 account of death on Mount Everest, *Into Thin Air*. Travel is like any other human enterprise: The potential is there for all manner of experiences, good and bad.

Below, in alphabetical order, are some of the writings and accounts most widely esteemed by discerning readers of travel books, from authors draped in legend to exponents, like Krakauer, of the new wave. Some of these authors speak to you directly across the ages, others from the day before yesterday. Making their acquaintance, and absorbing their insights, can't help but make your own travels richer.

Among the Russians by Colin Thubron (1983)
An Area of Darkness by V.S. Naipaul (1964, in India)
Arabian Sands by Wilfred Thesiger (1959)
As I Walked Out One Midsummer Morning by Laurie Lee (1969, in England)
The Beach by Alex Garland (a novel, 1996, on a backpacker's odyssey)
Black Lamb and Grey Falcon by Rebecca West (1941, in Yugoslavia)
Blue Highways by William Least-Heat Moon (1982, in the U.S.)
Coming into the Country by John McPhee (1977, in Alaska)
Coasting by Jonathan Raban (1987, Britain by sail)
Dark Star Safari by Paul Theroux (2002, in Africa)
Desert Solitaire by Edward Abbey (1968)
D.H. Lawrence and Italy edited by de Filippis, Eghghert and Kalnins (2008)
The End of the Game by Peter Beard (1965, in Africa)
Fear and Loathing in Las Vegas by Hunter S. Thompson (1971)
The Florida Keys by Joy Williams (1987)
From Sea to Sea by Rudyard Kipling (1899)
Ghost Train to the Eastern Star by Paul Theroux (2008)
Great Plains by Ian Frazier (1989)
The Great Railway Bazaar by Paul Theroux (1975)
Homage to Catalonia by George Orwell (1938, in Barcelona)
In Ethiopia with a Mule by Dervla Murphy (1968)
In Patagonia by Bruce Chatwin (1977)
The Innocents Abroad by Mark Twain (1869, into the Holy Lands)
Italian Hours by Henry James (1909, a novel of Venice)
Letters from Egypt: A Journey on the Nile, 1849–1850 by Florence Nightingale (1988)
The Lycian Shore by Freya Stark (1956, on the Turkish coast)
The Matter of Wales by Jan Morris (1984)
A Moveable Feast by Ernest Hemingway (1974, 2009 versions, in Paris)
Notes from a Small Island by Bill Bryson (1995, in England)
On the Road by Jack Kerouac (1957)
Our Man in Havana by Graham Greene (a novel, 1958)
Personal Narrative of a Pilgrimage to Al-Madinah & Meccah by Sir Richard Burton (1856)
The Rings of Saturn by W.G. Sebald (1992, in England)
The Road to Oxiana by Robert Byron (1937, in the Middle East)
Running the Amazon by Joe Kane (1989)

A Short Walk in the Hindu Kush by Eric Newby (1958, in Afghanistan)
Siren Land by Norman Douglas (1911, on the Isle of Capri)
The Snow Leopard by Peter Matthiessen (1978, on the Tibetan plateau in the Himalayas)
The Spanish Temper by V.S. Pritchett (1954)
The Tao of Travel: Enlightenments from Lives on the Road by Paul Theroux (2011)
Their Heads Are Green and Their Hands Are Blue by Paul Bowles (1963)
Thrilling Cities by Ian Fleming (1959)
Tracks by Robyn Davidson (1980, in Australia)
The Traveler's Tree: A Journey Through the Caribbean Islands by Patrick Leigh-Fermor (1950)
Travels by William Bartram (1791, in the Southeastern U.S.)
The Travels of Marco Polo (c.1300)
Travels with Charley by John Steinbeck (1962)
Travels With Myself and Another by Martha Gellhorn (1978)
Vagabonding: An Uncommon Guide to the Art of Long-Term World Travel by Rolf Potts (2002)
The Valley of the Assassins by Freya Stark (1934, in the Middle East)
Venice by Jan Morris (1960)
A Walk in the Woods by Bill Bryson (1998, on the Appalachian Trail)
West With the Night by Beryl Markham (a memoir, 1942)
Why We Travel by Pico Iyer (2000)
Wild Coast by John Gimlette (2011, into the Amazon)
A Year in Provence by Peter Mayle (1989)

Travel Story
Traveling with Books (2012)

> "No travel companion is likely to be richer, stranger, more
> alive and more eager to be intimate than a book."
> – Pico Iyer

Typically I travel solo, but I never go alone.

No, I always choose the best of traveling companions, engaging and unfailingly witty men and women with whom one need not compromise on what to do or where and when to do it. They do not insist that I rise at the crack of dawn or slip into slumber when the night life's just starting to hit its stride.

They do not demand I go shopping when I'm itching to hit the trail, explore a museum, take in a ball game or get pleasantly lost walking the streets of some unfamiliar city. And they can fit in a single bag. Or a Kindle or Nook, for that matter.

My steadfast compatriots on the road or in the skies are authors. Dead or alive, lofty or down to earth.

On a recent trip out West I was joined by Paul Theroux and Diane Ackerman, John D. MacDonald and Peter Mayle. Annie Dillard also made the journey, but got herself lost somewhere near West Thumb, Wyo.

The first rewarded me with a renewed sense of adventure, lending me his clear eye, keen observation, and a crackling prose style. The second offered fresh vistas, reminding me of her prodigious knowledge of the natural world — not least the human animal — and, more importantly, her remarkable grasp of its nuances, all in an irresistibly poetic voice.

The third ushered me back aboard the Busted Flush, Slip F-18, Bahia Mar, Fort Lauderdale, from which the ageless Travis McGee, that cynical though soft-centered "salvage specialist" still rights wrongs like a wire-haired knight errant.

The fourth suggests, most entertainingly, that the region of Provence in France, specifically the bucolic Luberon, is a meld of Tuscany and the working-class grit of Liverpool.

Not to say I spent every waking hour reading. Far from it, but these writers were always there when I wanted (or needed) the company, waiting patiently for my return, eager to talk to me, one to one. Sometimes, authors even speak to you across the centuries, their minds and voices still alive and vital, persuasive or captivating.

What could be better than reading E.M. Forster's "A Room With a View" while on a sojourn to Florence, Italy, where much of the story is set?

The beauty of it is that there is no end to the people you can ask to join you, year after year, nor any grumbling over last-minute substitutions. You don't even have to speak their language, since someone's already done you the service of translating.

Simply consult your bookshelves, if you still have them.

CHAPTER 16

Great Quotes on Travel

Great Quotes on Travel

Employing quotations has been dismissed by some as resorting to canned wisdom, the lazy writer's or conversationalist's way of masking his lack of originality by trotting out the ideas of others. But I disagree. The beauty of the quote is its gift of aphorism, a concise statement of a principle. And a writer should feel no compunction about borrowing them, judiciously if not excessively.

Many are simply impossible to resist, or improve upon, such as this aphoristic aside from Alexander von Humboldt: "The most dangerous worldview is the worldview of those who have not yet viewed the world."

In addition to those quotes that have graced the essays in this book, below are some of the most trenchant and memorable on travel I've come across over the years.

On the Move

"For my part, I travel not to go anywhere, but to go. I travel for travel's sake. The great affair is to move." — Robert Louis Stevenson, in *Travels with a Donkey in the Cevennes* (1879).

"Everyone ought to travel in the company of an artist. It is only when associated with one of this instructed class that a man discovers the use of his eyes, and begins to understand fully the beauties, and harmonies, and rich effects that pertain to so many things neglected by ordinary observers." — Oliver Bell Bunch in "Charleston and its Suburbs," *Appleton's Journal* (1871).

"To awaken quite alone in a strange town is one of the pleasantest sensations in the world." — Freya Stark in *Baghdad Sketches* (1932)

"There is no path to happiness. Happiness *is* the path." — attributed to Gautama Buddha

In Nature

"Climb the mountains and get their good tidings. Nature's peace will flow into you as sunshine flows into trees. The winds will blow their own freshness into you, and the storms their energy, while cares will drop off like autumn leaves." — John Muir in *Our National Parks* (1901)

"The love of wilderness is more than a hunger for what is always beyond our reach; it is also an expression of loyalty to the earth, the only home we shall ever know, the only paradise we ever need." — Edward Abbey, from a speech to environmentalists in Missoula, Mont. (1976)

"One touch of nature makes the whole world kin." — Shakespeare

"No more greater joy can come from life than to live inside a moment of adventure. It is the uncommon wilderness experience that gives your life expectation." — Frosty Wooldridge in *How to Live a Life of Adventure: The Art of Exploring the World* (2011)

"The attention of a traveler, should be particularly turned, in the first place, to the various works of Nature, to mark the distinctions of the climates he may explore, and to offer such useful observations on the different productions as may occur." — William Bartram in *Travels* (1791)

"It is not enough to fight for the land; it is even more important to enjoy it. While you can. While it's still there." — Edward Abbey, quoted in *Saving Nature's Legacy: Protecting and Restoring Biodiversity* (1994) by Reed F. Noss, Allen Y. Cooperrider, and Rodger Schlickeisen

"One climbs a mountain, not to conquer it, but to be lifted away from the earth up into the sky." — Russell Banks in *Voyages* (2016)

Going boldly

"One doesn't discover new lands without consenting to lose sight, for a very long time, of the shore." — Andre Gide in *Les faux-monnayeurs* (*The Counterfeiters*) (1925)

"Nobody can discover the world for somebody else. Only when we discover it for ourselves does it become common ground and a common bond and we cease to be alone." — Wendell Berry in *A Place on Earth* (1967)

"My course is set for an uncharted sea." — Dante Alighieri in *The Divine Comedy* (1321)

"Life begins at the end of your comfort zone." — Neale D. Walsch in *Conversations with God* (1995)

"All I ever wanted was a world without maps." — Michael Ondaatje in *The English Patient* (1996)

"Twenty years from now you will be more disappointed by the things you didn't do than by the ones you did do. So throw off the bowlines, sail away from the safe harbor. Catch the trade winds in your sails. Explore. Dream. Discover." — Attributed to Mark Twain in the April, 1998, New Yorker

"Following the sun, we left the old world." — inscription on Columbus' caravel (1492)

"Not all those who wander are lost." — J.R.R. Tolkien in *The Lord of the Rings*

"The gladdest moment in human life, me thinks, is a departure into unknown lands." — Sir Richard Burton quoted in *Captain Sir Richard Francis Burton: A Biography* by Edward Rice (2001)

"The world is a book, and those who do not travel read only one page." — variously attributed to Saint Augustine, but likely coined by Louis Charles Fougeret de Monbron in *Le Cosmopolite, ou, Le citoien de monde* (1750)

"One travels more usefully when alone, because he reflects more." — variously attributed to Thomas Jefferson

"Avoiding danger is no safer in the long run than outright exposure. The fearful are caught as often as the bold." — Helen Keller in *Let Us Have Faith* (1940)

"Life is not a journey to the grave with the intention to arrive safely in a pretty and well-preserved body; but rather to skid in broadside, thoroughly used up, totally worn out, and loudly proclaiming 'Wow! What a ride!'" — Hunter S. Thompson in *Hell's Angels* (1966)

"I see my path, but I don't know where it leads. Not knowing where I'm going is what inspires me to travel it." — Rosalia de Castro, quoted in *Where the Paved Road Ends* by Carolyn Han (2012)

"Do not follow where the path may lead. Go instead where there is no path and leave a trail." — Muriel Strode in the poem "Wind-Wafted Wild Flowers" (1903)

"I haven't been everywhere, but it's on my list." — Susan Sontag, in conversation

On being open

"The traveler sees what he sees, the tourist sees what he has come to see." — G.K. Chesterton in *The Temple Of Silence & Other Stories* (2013)

"The traveler was active; he went strenuously in search of people, of adventure, of experience. The tourist is passive; he expects interesting things to happen to him. He goes 'sight-seeing.'" — Daniel J. Boorstin in *The Image: A Guide to Pseudo-Events in America* (1961).

"To get lost is to learn the way." — African proverb

"If you wish to travel far and fast, travel light. Take off all your envies, jealousies, unforgiveness, selfishness and fears." — variously attributed to Cesare Pavese

"A mind that is stretched by a new experience can never go back to its old dimensions." — variously attributed to Oliver Wendell Holmes

"There are no foreign lands. It is the traveler only who is foreign." — Robert Louis Stevenson in *Travels with a Donkey in the Cevennes* (1879)

"The time you have left is a lifetime in itself. Use it well." — Michael Boiano, in conversation.

"A man grows tired while standing still." — Chinese proverb

"That great laborious tradition which produced genuine travel books – the eye slowly taking it all in, the aching feet imposing the leisure to observe the common people in the smoky inn kitchen." — Anthony Burgess, in his introduction to *Lawrence and Italy* (1972)

"When you travel, remember that a foreign country is not designed to make you comfortable. It is designed to make its own people comfortable." — Clifton Fadiman in *Clifton Fadiman's Fireside Reader* (1961)

What we gain

"To my mind, the greatest reward and luxury of travel is to be able to experience everyday things as if for the first time, to be in a position in which almost nothing is so familiar it is taken for granted." — Bill Bryson in *Down Under: Travels in a Sunburned Country* (2010)

"Travel is fatal to prejudice, bigotry and narrow-mindedness, and many of our people need it solely on those accounts. Broad, wholesome, charitable views of men and things cannot be acquired by vegetating in one little corner of the earth all one's life." — Mark Twain in *Innocents Abroad* (1869)

"The real voyage of discovery consists not in seeking new landscapes, but in having new eyes." — Marcel Proust in *Remembrance of Things Past* (1922)

"Once you have traveled, the voyage never ends, but is played out over and over again in the quietest chambers. The mind can never break off from the journey." — Attributed to Pat Conroy

"Our happiest moments as tourists always seem to come when we stumble upon one thing while in pursuit of something else." — Lawrence Block in *Write for Your Life* (1986)

"Travel does what good novelists also do to the life of everyday, placing it like a picture in a frame or a gem in its setting, so that the intrinsic qualities are made more clear." — Freya Stark in *Riding to the Tigris* (1959)

"We travel, some of us forever, to seek other places, other lives, other souls." — Anais Nin, quoted in *The Portable Anais Nin*, edited by Benjamin Franklin V (2010)

"Travel is at its most rewarding when it ceases to be about your reaching a destination and becomes indistinguishable from living your life." — Paul Theroux in *Ghost Train to the Eastern Star*

"Whereas the tourist generally hurries back home at the end of a few weeks or months, the traveler, belonging no more to one place than to the next, moves slowly, over periods of years, from one part of the earth to another." — Paul Bowles in *The Sheltering Sky* (1949)

"Stuff your eyes with wonder, live as if you'd drop dead in ten seconds. See the world. It's more fantastic than any dream made or paid for in factories." — Ray Bradbury in *Fahrenheit 451* (1953)

"All the pathos and irony of leaving one's youth behind is thus implicit in every joyous moment of travel: one knows that the first joy can never be recovered, and the wise traveler learns not to repeat successes but tries new places all the time." — Paul Fussell, quoted in *The Little Black Travel Journal* by Virginia Reynolds (2009)

"One's destination is never a place, but rather a new way of looking at things." — Henry Miller in the essay *Big Sur and the Oranges of Hieronymus Bosch* (1957)

Miscellaneous

"It is better to travel well than to arrive." — Attributed to Buddha

"Travel is the only thing you buy that makes you richer." — Anonymous

"Traveling – it leaves you speechless, then turns you into a storyteller." — Ibn Battuta, from the *Rilat Ibn Baūah (Journey of Ibn Battuta)*

"The whole object of travel is not to set foot on foreign land; it is at last to set foot on one's own country as a foreign land." — G.K. Chesterton in *Tremendous Trifles* (1909)

"When you're traveling, you are what you are right there and then. People don't have your past to hold against you. No yesterdays on the road." — William Least Heat Moon in *Blue Highways* (1982)

"Like all great travelers, I have seen more than I remember, and remember more than I have seen." — Benjamin Disraeli, quoted in *Wit and Wisdom of Benjamin Disraeli, Earl of Beaconsfield* (1881)

"I should like to spend the whole of my life in traveling abroad, if I could anywhere borrow another life to spend afterwards at home." — Attributed to

William Hazlitt

"The journey itself is my home." — Matsuo Bashō in *The Narrow Road to the Deep North and Other Travel Sketches* (English translation by Nobuyuki Yuasa, 1966)

"Don't tell me how educated you are, tell me how much you traveled." — Unknown. Attributed (spuriously) to Mohammed

"If you reject the food, ignore the customs, fear the religion and avoid the people, you might better stay at home." — Attributed to James Michener

"He who would travel happily must travel light." — Antoine de St. Exupery in *Wind, Sand and Stars* (1939)

"Certainly, travel is more than the seeing of sights; it is a change that goes on, deep and permanent, in the ideas of living." – Mary Ritter Beard in *America Through Women's Eyes* (1933)

"Travel and change of place impart new vigor to the mind." – Attributed to Seneca

"Life is either a daring adventure or nothing." – Helen Keller in *Let Us Have Faith* (1940)

"I have wandered all my life, and I have also traveled; the difference between the two being this, that we wander for distraction, but we travel for fulfillment." – Hilaire Belloc, quoted in *Lifetime Speaker's Encyclopedia* (1962) edited by Jacob Morton Braude

"There comes a moment on a journey when something sweet, something irresistible and charming as wine raised to thirsty lips, wells up in the traveler's being." – Patrick MacGill, quoted in *Children of the Dead End, The Autobiography of a Navvy*" by Herbert Jenkins (1914)

"Only by going alone in silence, without baggage, can one truly get into the heart of the wilderness. All other travel is mere dust and hotels and baggage and chatter." — Attributed to John Muir

"Luxury is the enemy of observation, a costly indulgence that induces such a good feeling that you notice nothing. Luxury spoils and infantilizes you and prevents you from knowing the world." — Paul Theroux, on high-gloss travel, in *Ghost Train to the Eastern Star*

"Now more than ever do I realize that I will never be content with a sedentary life, that I will always be haunted by thoughts of a sun-drenched elsewhere." — Isabelle Eberhardt, *The Nomad: The Diaries of Isabelle Eberhardt* (2003)

"I was here. I saw this, and it mattered to me." — Alain de Botton in *The Art of Travel* (2002)

And finally:

"We shall not cease from exploration, and the end of all our exploring will be to arrive where we started and know the place for the first time." — T. S. Eliot in *Little Gidding V, Four Quartets* (1943)

Afterword and Acknowledgements

It is my hope that this book will prove not only useful but edifying.

Until the Covid-19 virus struck in 2020, more people than ever were traveling the globe. According to the latest figures from the National Travel & Tourism office, there were 72,559,988 outbound trips from the U.S. in 2016, representing a 170% increase over a 20-year span. And that's just for Americans traveling abroad. This increase is driven largely by information, precisely the sort of information that *Why Travel?* augments and expands upon.

Despite the proliferation of blogs, apps and guidebooks that tell us where to go, what to see, eat, and do when we get there — tips that date quite rapidly — the most important questions about the topic of travel seldom are fully addressed. I flatter myself that I have provided some answers.

The virus that has disrupted our lives will pass. Travel will resume in all its manifestations.

I would like to thank everyone who has been instrumental in the completion and refining of this book. Chief among them are my former agent Nancy Barton for her expertise and advice, my editor Elise Gallagher for her sharp eye and suggestions, Jules Bond for her evocative book cover and formatting skills, old friend and fellow sojourner Ben Moise for his generous Foreword, and all the writers whose perceptiveness and skill have help extend my education on the subject, one supplemented by my own 40-plus years of travel. I also wish to thank P.J. Browning, publisher of *Charleston (S.C.) Post and Courier*, for granting permission to include previously published work in *Why Travel?*

Sine qua non.

Index of Attributions

In the Prologue:

"Travel, which was once either a necessity or an adventure, has become very largely a commodity, and from all sides we are persuaded into thinking that it is a social requirement, too." — Jan Morris in *In My Mind's Eye* (2018, W.W. Norton & Co.)

In *Traveling Solo*:

Likening random meetings to "four-minute swirls around a dance floor with different partners, little love affairs without consequences." — Willard Spiegelman in Senior Moments: Looking Back, Looking Ahead (2016)

In *On and Off the Beaten Path*

"A traveler doesn't know where he's going; a tourist doesn't know where he's been." — Paul Theroux in *The Tao of Travel* (2011)

The beaten path as "the crossroads of the world." — Doug Mack in *Europe on 5 Wrong Turns a Day* (2012)

In *Adventure Travel*

"At sunrise, it's not necessary, or even desirable, to know where you are going to be at sunset." — Dervla Murphy, quoted by Paul Theroux in *The Tao of Travel* (2011)

In *Glories of the Open Road*

"The open road is a beckoning, a strangeness, a place where a man can lose himself." — William Least Heat Moon in *Blue Highways* (1982)

In *The Spirit of Place*

On the art of literary travel writing dying out, "… transformed by a generation of writers concerned less with travel itself than with its deeper implications, places as ideas rather than facts." — Jan Morris in *In My Mind's Eye* (2018, W.W. Norton & Co.)

"The feeling that generations of emotion have left some vaporous sensation behind, perceptible still." — Jan Morris in *In My Mind's Eye* (2018)

"Walk as if you were kissing the earth with your feet." — Thich Nhat Hanh in *Call Me By My True Name* (1999)

"A good traveler returns exhilarated, restored, and confirmed by the jolt of strangeness. The most commonplace things are imbued with an exotic charge by the sheer fact of these varying degrees of unfamiliarity." — Willard Spiegelman *Senior Moments: Looking Back, Looking Ahead* (2016, Farrar, Straus and Giroux)

In *Places of the Heart*

"Here in the corner attic of America, two hours' drive from a rain forest, a desert, a foreign country, an empty island, a hidden fjord, a raging river, a glacier, and a volcano is a place where the inhabitants sense they can do no better, nor do they want to." Timothy Egan in *The Good Rain: Across Time & Terrain in the Pacific Northwest.*

In Traveling with Books

"No travel companion is likely to be richer, stranger, more alive and more eager to be intimate than a book." — Pico Iyer, quoted by Paul Theroux in *The Tao of Travel* (2011)

Photo Captions
(All photos by Bill Thompson, copyright Evening Post, Inc.)

1. Oia, the island of Santorini, Greece
2. Blackwater Falls in West Virginia
3. Chateau Frontenac, Quebec City, Canada
4. A cityscape of Prague, Czech Republic
5. On La Rambla in Barcelona, Spain
6. A bull elephant patrols his turf in South Africa
7. A verdant drive in Upper Michigan
8. The Temple of Poseidon at Cape Sounion, southern Greece
9. A quiet college campus in Munich, Germany
10. The charming Anafiotika neighborhood in Athens, Greece
11. Lake Mattamuskeet National Wildlife Refuge, North Carolina
12. Providence Canyon, Georgia
13. Antelope Canyon's sculpted walls, Arizona
14. Keukenhoff Gardens, Lisse, the Netherlands
15. Zion National Park, Utah
16. Sunset in the Aegean
17. A walk in the woods, near Lake Michigan
Cover photo: Perito Moreno glacier, Patagonia, Argentina

CPSIA information can be obtained
at www.ICGtesting.com
Printed in the USA
LVHW071425020321
680377LV00033B/320

9 781736 126400